# STORIES OF PRAISE

*Patrick and Donnalee Griffin*

IGNITE
PRESS
Fresno, CA

Published in the United States by
Ignite Press
5070 N. Sixth St. #189
Fresno, CA 93710
www.IgnitePress.us

ISBN: 978-1-953655-38-7 (Amazon Print)
ISBN: 978-1-953655-39-4 (IngramSpark) PAPERBACK
ISBN: 978-1-953655-40-0 (Ebook)

For bulk purchase and for booking, contact:

Fred Mendrin
FredSMendrin@gmail.com
Acts29Ministry.org

Unless otherwise noted, all scripture quotations are taken from the Holy Bible, New King James Version®. Copyright © 1982 by Thomas Nelson. Used by permission. All rights reserved.

Library of Congress Control Number: 2020925269

Cover design by Jibin Joy
Edited by Emma Hatcher
Interior design by Eswari Kamireddy

# CHAPTER 4

# CLING TO HIM IN PRAISE!

*"I will hope continually,*
*And will praise You yet more and more."*

—Ps. 71:14

## THE STORY

*I came up for my fifth parole hearing in June of 2010. By then, I had gone twenty-nine consecutive years with strong accomplishments (including multiple published books), and with no rule violations of any kind since my experience of Christ in 1981. I also had enormous outside support, including the friendship of a former director of the California prison system. This was Jim Rowland, who had brought the prisons under control after twenty-eight inmates were murdered in Folsom in 1986, and the mainlines all through the state were in an uproar with gang and racial violence. I met Jim through Fred Mendrin, after the two were introduced by a Prison Fellowship worker in Fresno. The friendship between Jim and Fred was an unlikely one, an ex-prison-gang member meeting the former director who did much to curb the influence of those gangs on the mainlines. But all things are possible with Christ, and, in 2009, through Fred's testimony of Christ's transforming work in me, Jim Rowland became interested in my situation. He, along with his beloved wife, Doris, began visiting and corresponding regularly, writing encouraging letters of wisdom and support. Also, through Fred I began receiving support and mentorship from Tom Sommers, a Christian business leader in Fresno. Tom had once been the executive director for the California Angels' farm club system, and had then worked as an executive for an insurance company. In retirement, he served as area director for the Christian Business Men's Connection, an association of Christian businessmen who connect with people individually for discipleship. Through phone calls and letters, Tom provided strong spiritual support and mentorship. Also, there was support from Joe Allio, a Christian with a unique and powerful testimony and a most beautiful family. Joe served his community as a police captain, and he would later be promoted to chief-of-police. He had begun visiting and corresponding with me in 2002, and a strong friendship had developed. This, and other support from the outside, combined with my decades of positive behavior on the inside, pointed to a promising outcome for the 2010 hearing.*

*About six weeks before the hearing, according to standard policy, I was interviewed by a forensic psychologist for what is called a Risk Assessment. The psychologist, based on the interview and on his reading of my central file, would recommend to the parole authorities his opinion on whether my risk to public safety was Low, Moderate, or High. This meant that when I sat before a Board of Prison Hearings panel for a decision on parole, if they had in front of them a Risk Assessment of Low, their mental profile of me would be positive before the hearing even*

# TABLE OF CONTENTS

# INTRODUCTION

This book was originally written as a collection of Bible Studies on the role of praise in the walk of faith, published under the title *Kings of Praise*. In this revision, we have simply added short, true-life stories, with each chapter divided into STORY and BIBLE STUDY sections. In the final chapter, the order is reversed, with the story following the Bible Study.

Part I consists of five chapters, with stories from the life of the lead-author, Patrick Griffin. Part II consists of one chapter with a story from the life of Fred Mendrin, whose brief bio is included. Part III consists of two chapters, with stories from the life of co-author, Donnalee Griffin.

Special thanks and recognition goes to Carlos Aceves, who was instrumental in shaping the original collection of Bible Studies.

This book emphasizes what the scripture itself teaches on the role of praise in worship and spiritual warfare and also how the history recorded in the Bible was "written for our learning, that we through the patience and comfort of the Scriptures might have hope" (Rom 15:4, emphasis added). The personal stories are offered as present-day examples of how God inhabits the praises of His people and how praise is a bold expression of the faith by which all things become possible.

# PART I

## A STORY FROM PATRICK'S LIFE

# CHAPTER 1
# REJOICE IN HIS WORD!

*"They believed His words;*
*They sang His praise."*

—Ps. 106:12

## THE STORY

*This part of my story begins at age twenty-three. I had been incarcerated since 1979, having entered the prison system at age twenty-one with a combined sentence of eight years for two counts of assault-with-deadly-weapon. The prisons in those times were largely out of control with inmate-on-inmate aggression, and from the beginning I chose a policy of survival through violence as my option of first resort. This led to the commission of three additional crimes involving prison-made weapons during my first two years, and for these acts of violence I received additional sentences of three years, seven years, and twenty-five-years-to-life.*

*In March of 1981, I stabbed to death an inmate on the mainline of the prison in Vacaville. My mind had sunk so deep into the decadence of crime that I believed I had good reasons for committing the act, and afterward my conscience troubled me no more than if I had stepped on a fly. Three months later, in a part of the prison called administrative segregation, one night, alone in my cell, I fell into a powerful depression that brought me to the decision of taking my own life. In the darkness after lights-out, with no other sound on the wing except the fading bootsteps of a guard making his final rounds, I pulled a sheet from my bed and began shaping it into a noose. Right at that time, something happened. I had not been praying, and God had been nowhere in my thoughts, but suddenly His favor fell upon me, unasked for and unexpected. Instead of going up to the vent with the noose, I went down to the floor on my knees. One moment, I had been thinking only of escape through death, and the next moment, I was aware of nothing except my guilt and condemnation before God.*

*For a long time I stayed there, on my knees with my face pressed into the cement, and I do not recall having anything in my awareness except the numbness of fear, dread, and shame. After some time, I do not know how long, a new idea rushed into my mind, along with a powerful emotion. Somehow, suddenly, I knew that all of my problems with God, and with everything else, are resolved in Jesus Christ. I could not have explained this at the time, but I knew it with absolute certainty.*

*After a minute, I rose to my feet and looked around my cell. Everything was the same, but the way I looked at everything was different. I knew that by clinging to Jesus Christ I was safe from every threat, including the threats of shame and condemnation. I felt a peace that was deeper than any other feeling, and I calmly picked up the sheet and remade my bed, then got into it and fell asleep. When I woke up in the morning, the peace was still there. Christ was still there. I was twenty-three years old, and God had* met me at the edge to snatch me away from final destruction. I do not know of any person who was more undeserving of this than me. What fell upon me that night was pure mercy, unearned and undeserved. Through His Son Jesus Christ, by a sovereign act of His Holy Spirit, God had given me the bath I needed, and He had put into me something that was not there before.

Although my criminal history had been extreme and had included a prior term in a youth prison for armed robbery with a gun, and although I was an out of control, violent criminal, since that night of experiencing the fear of God, and the beauty and power of Jesus Christ as my Lord and Savior, I became a different person.

That is how my change came about. There is no other factor, no other influence, and no other source that can rightly be given even the least of the credit. Jesus Christ the Son of God gets all the credit, all the glory, all the praise.

From that night in 1981, I began a new life that remained drug-free, alcohol-free, and violence-free. On April 5, 1982, only thirteen months after committing a murder, the prison authorities released me back to the same mainline with full program privileges. This was not normal policy, but it showed that Christ turns the hearts of authorities in whatever ways He chooses, and He is able to arrange the most unlikely developments. Following the Lord Jesus Christ, with faith that defies one's own understanding, is a life of surprises. But it would take me a long time to learn that sometimes the surprises are devastating. And it would take a long time for my confidence in my own understanding to be truly crushed so that I could learn to rely more boldly on the wisdom and power of God.

The years passed, and I became eligible for parole in 1994. At that initial hearing, I was rightly denied by the California Board of Prison Hearings (BPH). After that, I was again denied parole at a hearing in 1998, and again in 2002, and again in 2005. Shortly after that fourth denial, I was visited at the prison in San Luis Obispo by my close and longtime friend, Fred Mendrin.

Fred is a former California prisoner who had entered the system in 1970 with a sentence of six months to ten years for possession of half-an-ounce of marijuana. During his first several years of incarceration, Fred committed multiple violent crimes against other inmates, including a gang-related murder in 1972. Fred was a member of a prison gang called the Aryan Brotherhood. In 1978, while alone in his cell in the same prison where he had brutally taken the life of another man, Fred experienced faith in Jesus Christ as his Lord and Savior. From that day, he became a different person, committed to a life that would honor his Lord who had died for him and rose again. Fred never again returned to drugs or alcohol or violence, or to a criminal lifestyle in any way. I met him in 1982, about a year after my experience of salvation. From the day we met, at a table in a dining room less than an hour after my release back to the mainline, a bond of friendship and brotherhood began to form. After Fred paroled in 1985, he continued to support me with a friendship that I can best describe as epic. He visited me in every prison, often bringing his wife and daughters. In 2002, when my mom died suddenly from a brain aneurysm at age sixty, Fred drove 500 miles round trip from Fresno to Anaheim, to stand with my family in my place during that time of pain and loss. He is that kind of a friend.

So, in 2005, at the prison in San Luis Obispo, after my fourth parole denial, Fred came to tell me of his intention to raise money for a lawyer. He believed the right attorney could get my case back in court and have the controlling charge reduced from first-degree murder to voluntary manslaughter, meaning that, if successful, I would be released at once with time served. Fred assured me there were strong legal grounds for mounting such an appeal (due to known, mitigating circumstances surrounding the crime), and I gave the go-ahead. After the visit, Fred spoke with a Fresno attorney who looked through my case and assured us that he could get me out of prison, with time served on a lesser charge. Fred raised $10,000 to pay the attorney, and he would eventually raise another $15,000. The process took some time, but on August 17, 2007, my fiftieth birthday, the attorney came to visit me in the Soledad prison, to personally hand me a copy of the writ.

As I took into my hands the thick packet with a bright red cover, the attorney said to me, "This one is a slam dunk." My experience at hearing those words was dreamlike. I felt amazement at the assuring thought of my case being brought back to court. The attorney then assured me I would be out of prison in less than a year, on an unconditional release with no parole. As I stared at the face of this experienced attorney, listening to him speak in a matter-of-fact tone, I saw no reason for doubting his words. He seemed as though he very much knew what he was talking about, and I walked out of the room believing that within a year I would be out of prison and at home with my family. I did not feel I deserved any of this, but I saw it as an act of mercy from God, a most kind and wonderful gift of grace on my fiftieth birthday.

After meeting with the attorney, I walked down the cement staircase leading to the corridor, feeling like a child waking up on Christmas morning. After a guard unlocked the door, I stepped into the crowded, noisy corridor and felt the blast of heat from that hot summer day. As I walked toward my wing, everything around me was the same as before—the suffocating crowd of inmates and guards in a densely overpopulated prison, the smell of hot cement, a hundred people all talking at the same time—everything was the same, but I felt a pleasant buffer between me and the ugly world around me. That buffer was the refuge of assurance that I would soon be delivered from this decades-long nightmare of rightly deserved imprisonment.

All through the day I carried in my mind a sweet delight, and when evening came, I went to the yard. At the Soledad Central Facility, the yard stretches out about two-hundred yards in each direction, and in the cool of the evening I walked alone on the dirt track alongside the fence. Through the wire fence, I looked out at the surrounding fields, at the trees, the rolling hills, the flowers, and the passing cars on nearby Highway 101. I felt delightfully astonished at the thought that I, the most unworthy person I know, would soon have opportunity to show the outside world what Jesus Christ had done for me, how He changed me, and what I was prepared to do for honoring His name through a life of witness and service.

The night passed, and when I woke up in the morning I felt I was living in a different world. For the next four months I carried within myself a deep excitement and expectation of wonderful things to come. My family and outside supporters also rejoiced and were counting the days. One night in December, a very cold night, I went out to the yard, knowing that few inmates would go out because of the unusual cold. Normally there is a line at the phones, but on that night I was able to go directly to the nearest one and call my sister, Pam. The attorney had told Fred that my case could be reviewed at the initial phase on any day, so when Pam answered my call, and as we talked, she called Fred in the hope that he had heard something. I could not hear what Fred was saying, but I listened expectantly to Pam's voice as she related his words from the attorney. The words were short and to the point, and for a moment I struggled to process what I had just heard. She had said, "The writ was **denied**."

Imagine flying on an airplane on a beautiful summer day and

*that you do not see the mountain. In one second, the sweet ex-pectation that I had carried for months fell to the ground and shattered. I thought of how hard this would be for Pam and the rest of our family, and I thought of all the work that Fred had done and the cost. It seemed that, after twenty-eight years in pris-on, I had been brought to the gate in the expectation of release, and then abruptly told that it was not to be.*

*Although the news hit me hard, within seconds I heard and felt in my spirit the words of scripture, saying with authority:*

"Call upon **Me** in the day of trouble; I will deliver you, and you shall glorify Me."

—Ps. 50:15

*Immediately behind that, like another strong wave rising up from within, I heard and felt the words:*

"Cast your burden on the Lord, And He shall sustain you."

—Ps. 55:22

*After finishing the call with Pam, I walked out on the grass and looked up at the sky. In a prison, because of the surround-ing lights, no one can see stars. I had not seen stars for nearly thirty years. I stood there a while, alone in the cold and staring up at a dark sky. Then, I said to God something like, "Father, I don't see the stars . . . but I know they are there." I lowered my eyes and looked around, and all that I could see was ugliness. The gun towers, the searchlights, the razor wire along the tops of the high, double fences. Everything looked dreary, and I felt hopelessness pressing against my mind like a tightening vice. I watched an inmate walking with his hands in his pockets as he passed by a tower, and I saw the steam of his breath in the glare of the lights. Then, I looked again to the sky and began to pray, and I kept praying, offering to God all of my pain and fear and uncertainty. As I continued clinging to Him in prayer, I felt in my spirit a surge of passion and resolve to find triumph for Christ's glory through this turn of events. The chapters of this book are one result.*

## BIBLE STUDY

Are your circumstances harsh and the difficulties accumulating? If so, you can triumph through God's favor by placing joyful praise ahead of everything. Rejoicing in the face of staggering problems is not a denial of the legitimacy of life's concerns (finances, health, troubled relationships, loss of a loved one); rather, it is a confession of confidence in the faithfulness of God to provide what is needed for those who come boldly. The following study will show you from scripture how the power of God works through faith expressed in joyful praise.

\* \* \* \*

When the angel Gabriel delivered God's word to Mary, saying, "you will conceive in your womb and bring forth a Son," the virgin did not waver in unbelief but rather said to the heavenly messenger:

> "Behold, the maidservant of the Lord! Let it be to me according to Your word."
>
> —Luke 1:31, 38

For a virgin to bring forth a child is no less a miracle than for a dead person to rise from the grave. The Old Testament provides at least two examples of the dead rising by God's power, but no one before Mary had ever witnessed a virgin giving birth. As with Abraham and Sarah when entrusted with a remarkable promise, Mary also "did not waver at the promise of God through unbelief, but was strengthened in faith, giving glory to God, and being fully convinced that what He had promised He was also able to perform" (Rom. 4:20–21).

After Mary had received the word, she "went into the hill country with haste, to a city of Judah, and entered the house of Zacharias and greeted Elizabeth" (Luke 1:39–40)," who said to Mary:

"Blessed is she who believed, for there will be a fulfillment of those things which were told her from the Lord."
—Luke 1:45

Mary, who at that early time would have felt no physical signs of pregnancy, did not wait for visible evidence before rejoicing and praising God:

"And Mary said: 'My soul magnifies the Lord, And my spirit has rejoiced in God my Savior . . . Henceforth all generations will call me blessed. For He who is mighty has done great things for me, and holy is His name.'"
—Luke 1:46–49

Like Sarah before her, Mary needed no visible evidence before rejoicing in the word of the promise. As the scripture testifies of Sarah:

"By faith Sarah herself also received strength to conceive seed, and she bore a child when she was past the age, because she judged Him faithful who had promised."

—Heb. 11:11

Both of these women received fruit in the womb when they joyfully confessed that "with God nothing will be impossible" (Luke 1:37).

Does your own life feel like an empty womb? If so, you can fill all of your emptiness by the one sure step of rejoicing in the word of God. Rather than waiting for visible evidence of blessing, remember the scripture that tells us that "the desert shall rejoice and blossom as the rose" (Isa. 35:1b). The natural mind is conditioned to wait for the blossom before having joy, but the mind of faith boldly rejoices when the season is still dry. As Jesus testified of Abraham, who was promised a Son whom he saw only through the eye of faith:

"Your father Abraham rejoiced to see My day, and he saw it and was glad."

—John 8:56

Jesus, whom the scripture identifies as "the Son of Abraham" (Matt. 1:1), was born about eighteen centuries after the word of the promise was given. But Abraham rejoiced so completely in the word that he enjoyed the day of Christ while living long before His birth.

For Abraham and Sarah, as with Mary after them, the rejoicing of faith preceded the blossom of the desert, and all these things were "written for our learning" (Rom. 15:4).

However dry or threatening your life situation may seem, these biblical examples and exhortations were written for your encouragement and wisdom in the faith. Do not underestimate the relevance of these examples to your own life. "All things are possible to him who believes" (Mark 9:23), and by constantly rejoicing in the word of the Lord, you will purify your heart from the doubt that hinders "the power of God through faith" (1 Pet. 1:5). The Lord "is able to do exceedingly abundantly above all that we ask or think" (Eph. 3:20), and even the threat of death becomes a slave to the welfare of those who rejoice with confidence in the word of the living God.

When the prophet Jeremiah was hunted by "the men of Anathoth" (Jer. 11:21) who had devised a scheme to "cut him off from the land of the living" (11:19), the prophet cried out to God and asked:

"Why does the way of the wicked prosper?"
—12:1

The Lord acknowledged to Jeremiah that those who wrongly persecuted him "have dealt treacherously with you, yes, they have called a multitude after you" (12:6). But the situation did not improve for the complaining man of God, who later said:

"Woe is me, my mother, that you have borne me, A man of strife and a man of contention to the whole earth!"
—15:10a

It seemed to Jeremiah that the whole world was pressing against him, and that "every one of them curses me" (15:10b). Do you know this feeling? Does it seem that nothing is working the way it should and your life is an impossible burden? Is your neighborhood flooded with gang and criminal activity, and do you fear for your children's vulnerability to the corrupting influences? If any of these are a threat to you, you can flee to the remedy that Jeremiah found when surrounded by hatred and violence:

> "Your words were found, and I ate them, And Your word was to me the joy and rejoicing of my heart; For I am called by Your name, O LORD God of hosts."
>
> —15:16

By rejoicing in the Lord's word, we wrap our lives into His name, and there is no greater way to call on His name than to rejoice in His word. As the scripture tells us in the Psalms:

> "You have magnified Your word above all Your name."
>
> —138:2

By rejoicing in His word, we come to the refuge of His name:

> "You are my hiding place and my shield; I hope in Your word."
>
> —Ps. 119:114

The scripture tells us that "the word of God is living and powerful" (Heb. 4:12), and that man shall live "by every word of God" (Luke 4:4). Only the mind of faith can sink its teeth into this word and drink its power, and nothing is impossible for those who believe without doubting. There is a faith that merely gets by, but if you want the faith that moves mountains, you will say with the psalmist:

> "I rejoice at Your word As one who finds great treasure."
>
> —Ps. 119:162

When a person finds a great treasure, his heart leaps with excitement, and he thinks of the way this treasure will change his life. According to Jesus, "if you have faith and do not doubt," your life will change so dramatically that "nothing will be impossible for you" (Matt. 21:21; 17:20). To fully experience the treasure of God's word, all we need is a drop of pure faith:

> "[I]f you have faith as a mustard seed, you will say to this mountain, 'Move from here to there,' and it will move; and nothing will be impossible for you."
>
> —Matt. 17:20

Is your heart afflicted by the impurities of doubt? Is unbelief hindering your experience of the living power of God's word? A remedy for the doubting heart is to rejoice with constant praise in the treasure of the word. As the psalmist confessed in another place:

> "Your testimonies . . . are the rejoicing of my heart."
>
> —119:111

> "I have rejoiced in the way of Your testimonies, As much as in all riches."
>
> —119:14

"The word of the LORD is proven" (Ps. 18:30), and we should boldly rejoice in the unshakeable certainty of His "exceedingly great and precious promises" (2 Pet. 1:4). The Lord has given us a treasure that will transform our lives and empower us to walk on water if needed, but this treasure remains largely untapped until we seize the word with aggressive rejoicing that annihilates doubt.

Those who have the faith that moves mountains do not wring their hands and mumble their confession like a whimpering sigh. Even in the worst of times, an aggressive believer will "rejoice before You according to the joy of harvest, as men rejoice when they divide the spoil" (Isa. 9:3). The visible world can intimidate the natural eye, but the rejoicing believer stands in awe of God's word:

"Princes persecute me without a cause, But my heart stands in awe of Your word."

—Ps. 119:161

The word of God, which brought the universe into existence and holds it together, is "living and powerful" and worthy of our joyful confidence. As David confessed in a song after his enemies had captured him:

"Whenever I am afraid, I will trust in You. In God (I will praise His word), In God I have put my trust; I will not fear. What can flesh do to me?"

—Ps. 56:3–4

We note that David did not sing this song from a place of physical safety and comfort. The Philistines had "captured him in Gath" (Ps. 56:1), but David filled his heart with the treasure of God's word and left no room in his thoughts for the cancer of doubt.

The biblical history of David's life shows a man who triumphed through joy. In his many adversities, and sometimes against staggering odds, he "strengthened himself in the LORD his God" by offering songs of praise (cf. 1 Sam. 30:6; Ps. 56:13; 27:1). For seventeen years, he ran for his life, hiding in caves and wandering through deserts, all the while composing psalms expressing his joyful confidence in the mercy and faithfulness of God. By songs of joyful praise, David fixed his mind on the Lord, providing us with a living example of the scripture that tells us, "You will keep him in perfect peace, Whose mind is stayed on You" (Isa. 26:3). Faith and rejoicing link profoundly in the scriptures, as in the following verse:

> "But let all those rejoice who put their trust in You; Let them ever shout for joy."
> —Ps. 5:11a

Faith without rejoicing is common, but this is not a biblical faith. As David tells us again in another Psalm:

> "For our heart shall rejoice in Him, because we have trusted in His holy name."
> —33:21

But where there is no rejoicing, our faith will limp and stagger. A failure to rejoice places a person outside the will of God, as the scripture makes clear in the following passage:

> "Rejoice always, pray without ceasing, in everything give thanks; for this [continuous prayer with joyful thanksgiving] is the will of God in Christ Jesus for you."
> —1 Thess. 5:16–18, brackets added

By continual rejoicing, we abide in the Lord's will and set fire to faith for the burning away of doubt.

When Paul drew near to Jerusalem for the last time, knowing that chains and tribulations awaited him, he spoke to the

Christians about his resolve to "finish my race with joy" (Acts 20:22–24). Without the fuel of joy, our faith will struggle to endure, so the apostle exhorts us again and again to "rejoice in the Lord always" (Phil. 4:4). The Book of Hebrews was written to Christians enduring harsh and prolonged affliction, and the scripture exhorts them to "hold fast to the confidence and rejoicing of the hope firm to the end" (Heb. 3:6). These Christians "joyfully accepted the plundering of [their] goods," and they were assured that by steadfast rejoicing "firm to the end," they would "imitate those who by faith and patience inherit the promises" (10:34, 6:12).

Our joyfulness expresses adoration, gratitude, and confidence in Christ as our Shepherd and King. This joyfulness is not dependent on circumstances, as Paul testified in a letter written from a prison cell in Rome:

> "I thank my God . . . always in every prayer of mine making request for you all with joy . . . I shall remain and continue with you all for your progress and joy of faith . . . I am glad and rejoice with you all . . . Finally, my brethren, rejoice in the Lord . . . rejoice in Christ Jesus . . . Rejoice in the Lord always. Again I will say, Rejoice!"
> —Phil. 1:3–4, 25–26; 3:1; 4:4b

From his vile circumstance, he magnified God with continual rejoicing, testifying that "I have learned in whatever state I am, to be content" (4:11). If we aim for the triumph that Paul experienced, we will rejoice as Paul rejoiced. As he said to us all by the authority of the Spirit:

> "I urge you, imitate me."
> —1 Cor. 4:16

Whatever is going on in your life, you can seize the upper hand by an instant, one-step leap into a lifestyle of aggressive praise with joyful thanksgiving. You can do this at all times. You can do this in all situations. You can do this right now.

We know from scripture that "the word of the LORD is proven" (Ps. 18:30), but the scripture also tells us:

"If you will not believe, Surely you shall not be established."
—Isa. 7:9b

How do we deal with unbelief? We vaporize it with joy. As the prophet Habakkuk also confessed, in a song recorded for our learning:

"Though the fig tree may not blossom, Nor fruit be on the vine; Though the labor of the olive may fail, And the field yield no food; Though the flock may be cut off from the fold, And there be no herd in the stalls—yet I will rejoice in the LORD, I will joy in the God of my salvation. The LORD God is my strength; He will make my feet like deer's feet, And He will make me walk on my high hills."
—Hab. 3:17–19

By *rejoicing* in the Lord's strength, we *walk* in His strength, and we can do this when the cupboards are empty and the bank account is dry. Regardless of the severity of our circumstances, and regardless of what threatens us, the scripture commands us to cast our burden on the Lord by joyfully giving praise at all times:

"Rejoice in the Lord always . . . be anxious for nothing."
—Phil 4:4a; 4:6a

These two sayings connect. We cannot have the one without the other. By aggressive, continuous rejoicing in the word of the Lord, no room is left in the heart for the burden of anxiety.

By joyfully giving praise, we give the Lord our burden, and every new burden becomes an immediate cause for rejoicing in a new opportunity for God to show Himself faithful. With so much scriptural exhortation, and with so many biblical examples, we should not hesitate to cast our burden on the Lord by rejoicing in the treasure of His word. "Has He said, and will He not do? Or has He spoken, and will He not make it good?" (Num. 23:19). In the flesh, we may feel weak and insufficient, but the scripture assures us from beginning to end that, by rejoicing in His word, we will triumph through the favor of His name.

# CHAPTER 2

# PRAISE GOD!

*"Therefore by Him let us continually offer the
sacrifice of praise to God."*

—HEB. 13:15a, EMPHASIS ADDED

## THE STORY

*On that December night, I came in from the yard at the mandatory, 8:30 recall. On my face I felt the warmth coming off the
radiators lining the corridor walls, but the cold of the outside still
clung to me through my clothing and the memory of what I had
just experienced. Learning of the denial had powerfully changed
the way my brain was working, from a delightful excitement of expectation to one of uncertainty, pain, and helplessness. The walk
from the yard to my wing was long, more than two-hundred yards,
and as I passed wing after wing, glancing through the doorways
to see crowds of inmates in each dayroom, I tried to process the
new knowledge that I would not be leaving this environment any
time soon, maybe not ever.*

*Since coming into prison at age twenty-one, I had already lost my dearly loved mother, and the experience of hearing the news of her passing left me always aware that a mind-shattering word can come at the most unexpected moment. Mom was only sixty, and her sudden death caught all of us off guard. After getting the dark news on that sunny summer day, I went to my cell and cried for five hours, uncontrollably. From that time, with passion and frequency, I expressed to my heavenly Father, in the name of Jesus at His right hand, a longing, clinging request that He would not permit my aged father to leave this world without seeing me on the land where he lived. Growing old in prison is a drip, drip, drip of agony, always wondering when the next hard news from home will come. A car crash, a disease, a heart attack, another person from my history gone from the earth, and I cannot be there even to stand with my family at a funeral. These were the kind of thoughts weighing heavy on my soul as I walked from the yard to my cell at the far end of the prison.*

*After reaching my wing, I climbed the staircase to the third floor, where I waited near my cell for the nighttime lockup. With my forearms resting on the steel bars that run along the edge of the tier, I looked down at the noisy crowd of inmates milling about in the dayroom. Just a couple hours earlier, I had believed that I would soon be away from all of this. My emotions swayed like a pendulum, or better, they lurched up and down like a jolting seesaw. First, the downward, gripping pull of grief and disappointment, and then the shift upward to a focus on Christ, knowing that with Him all things are possible for those who believe. Then, a minute later, the downward yank.*

*Just before nine o'clock, the bell rang, and an officer pulled a bar near the front of the wing to unlock all of the doors. By God's grace, I had what is called a single cell, meaning I did not have a cellmate. I stepped inside and closed the door behind* me while looking around at the familiar room where I spent so much of my life. A few seconds later, the heavy lock on the door slammed into place with a sickening thud, and then there was silence. In that moment, I felt so very grateful to be alone.

After changing into more comfortable clothes, I started my pace, from the back window to the door. Three steps this way, three steps back. This went on for a long time, back and forth, back and forth. I clung to the presence of the Lord, not knowing what to ask, just gripping my Shepherd by faith and casting on Him all my uncertainties, fears, anguish, and sorrow. I had taken a good life and destroyed it, along with so badly damaging the welfare and happiness of others. With fifty years now behind me, I wondered where it all was going? My life on this earth, what would it come to in the end? Would I someday die of old age in prison? Would my testimony of Jesus ever amount to anything beyond the prison walls, or was my failure as a human being the final word about me? At some point, during those hours of pacing, clinging, and confessing that I did not know what to do, a passage of short verses rose up in my mind. I felt the force of wisdom and power in the living words that say:

"Rejoice always, pray without ceasing, in everything give thanks; for THIS is the will of God in Christ Jesus for you."
—1 Thess. 5:16–18, emphasis added

I stopped pacing, and I fixed my mind entirely on this inner voice instructing me to joyfully give thanks without ceasing, not at some later time, under more pleasant circumstances, but NOW. The verses told me clearly that THIS is God's will for me *in Christ Jesus. I had been confessing that "I don't know what to do," but now, without any doubt, I knew exactly what to do.*

*In the shadows and silence of my cell, I bowed on my knees between the locker and the commode, and with my face to the wall I said something like, "Father, I give You thanks for the denial of the writ, and for all that You will accomplish for Your glory in my life through this experience." As I brought that confession to God, I knew He had given me the grace to truly mean what I was saying. From that moment, my spiritual walk with Jesus Christ rose to a new height.*

# BIBLE STUDY

Whatever your situation, whatever the odds against you or the severity of the threat, God has provided a tested and proven advantage. Praise is identified in scripture as a weapon of warfare guaranteed to defeat what opposes the glory of God in your life. The scripture in Psalms speaks of how believers will "triumph in Your praise" (106:47), and the following study will show you from scripture how praising God is the proven way to experience the Lord's power for triumph in every situation.

\*   \*   \*   \*

Praise is identified in scripture as an offering of worship and a weapon of war:

"Whoever offers praise glorifies Me."

—Ps. 50:23a

"Through the praise of children and infants you have established a stronghold against your enemies, to silence the foe and the avenger."

—Ps. 8:2, NIV: cf. Matt. 21:16

Are your circumstances harsh and the difficulties accumulating? If so, you can triumph through God's favor by placing the weapon of joyful praise ahead of everything. Without leaving other things undone, rejoice in the faithfulness of God by putting praise ahead of every effort, every prayer, every thought. The Bible is loaded with exhortations and historical examples of God's power working through the praise of His people, and we have no reason for doubting His involvement through our praises today.

Six centuries before the birth of Jesus, when Jehoshaphat reigned as king over Judah, an assembly of Gentile armies invaded the homeland of God's people. The Book of Second Chronicles records how "the people of Moab with the people of Ammon, and others with them besides the Ammonites, came to battle against Jehoshaphat. Then some came and told Jehoshaphat, saying, 'A great multitude is coming against you' " (20:1–2). The passage records that "Jehoshaphat feared, and set himself to seek the LORD" (20:3). After the king had assembled his people in Jerusalem, he prayed aloud in the temple court:

"O LORD God . . . we have no power against this great multitude that is coming against us; nor do we know what to do, but our eyes are upon You."

—20:6, 12

In reading this biblical history, we should not remain bystanders, passively watching. We want to enter spiritually into the situation and learn for ourselves a lesson in the art of war against great opposition. Who among us, believers in Christ on the earth today, can fail to identify with the feeling expressed by Jehoshaphat in his impossible situation? In times of great distress, when the difficulties accumulate and we feel overwhelmed by all that comes against us, we can say with Jehoshaphat in our prayer to God: "I have no power against all that is coming against me, nor do I have the wisdom to know what to do" (20:12).

But in our helplessness, we can glorify God by fighting with the weapon used by Jehoshaphat:

> "And when he had consulted with the people, he appointed those who should sing to the LORD, and who should praise the beauty of holiness, as they went out before the army and were saying: 'Praise the LORD, for His mercy endures forever.'"
>
> —20:21

With no strength or wisdom of his own, the king placed all his care in the hand of God by concentrating on praise. The next verse shows us what happens when the Lord's people put praise ahead of everything:

> "Now when they began to sing and to praise, the LORD set ambushes against the people of Ammon, Moab, and Mount Seir, who had come against Judah; and they were defeated."
>
> —20:22

By placing praise ahead of every concern, the people of Judah laid hold on "the power of God through faith" for deliverance and triumph against impossible odds.

The scripture tells us that God has "ordained praise . . . to silence the foe" (Ps. 8:2). We know that God is faithful to His word, and we know He is "the same yesterday, today, and forever" (Heb. 13:8). If He acted through the praise of His people yesterday, why should we think that He will fail to act through the praise of His people today? The scripture says that we will "triumph in Your praise," and whoever lives for God's praise through faith in His Son is guaranteed the triumph in all times and all situations. As the scripture assures us again in Second Corinthians:

> "Now thanks be to God who always leads us in triumph in Christ."
>
> —2:14a

And again in First Corinthians:

> "But thanks be to God, who gives us the victory through our Lord Jesus Christ."
>
> —15:57

We have read the account of the Lord's intervention through the praise of His people in the days of Jeshoshaphat, and we can use our imaginations to see the singers marching before the army, marching to the battle with the voice of praise as their weapon of choice. The scripture in Romans tells us that "whatever things were written before were written for our learning" (Rom. 15:4), and what we learn from Jehoshaphat is that those who commit their lives to praising God will triumph through the power of His name.

Knowing this, should we not heed the word that tells us to "continually offer the sacrifice of praise to God" (Heb. 13:15)?

Help is promised in time of need for those who come to God

boldly: "Let us therefore come boldly to the throne of grace, that we may obtain mercy and find grace to help in time of need" (Heb. 4:16, emphasis added). In times of need, those who come with joyful praise show the boldness of faith that lays hold on the promise and does not let go.

Another example of spiritual boldness is David's attitude of praise while running for his life in the Judean wilderness. David spent seventeen years in his wanderings, rejoicing through laughter and tears, singing to God in the darkest hour and saying:

"You number my wanderings; Put my tears into Your bottle; Are they not in Your book? When I cry out to You, Then my enemies will turn back; This I know, because God is for me. In God (I will praise His word), In the LORD (I will praise His word), In God I have put my trust; I will not be afraid. What can man do to me?"

—Ps. 56:8–11

David wrote this psalm after he had been captured by the enemy Philistines while running for his life from Saul. Rather than yielding to doubt and voicing complaints in unbelief, he offered songs of praise to boldly confess his confidence in God. David did not deny his pain or the dreadful opposition surrounding him; yet, by mingling his tears with joyful praise, he obtained the help that God has promised to those who come boldly.

If the scriptures clearly establish praise as a means of triumph by God's power in Christ, why should we hesitate to praise Him continuously in even our toughest situations?

For those who walk by faith, the major enemy is doubt. The Lord Jesus, after He had caused a fig tree to wither, said:

"Assuredly, I say to you, if you have faith and do not doubt, you will not only do what was done to the fig tree, but also if you say to this mountain, Be removed and be cast into the sea, it will be done. And whatever things you ask in prayer, believing, you will receive."

—Matt. 28:21–22

This remarkable saying shows that nothing is impossible for those who "have faith and do not doubt." But how do we drive from our minds the doubt that hinders our experience of God's power and the fullness of His favor?

When the apostles said to the Lord, "Increase our faith," Jesus answered: "If you have faith as a mustard seed, you can say to this mulberry tree, 'Be pulled up by the roots and be planted in the sea,' and it would obey you . . . and nothing will be impossible for you" (Luke 17:5–6; Matt. 17:20). What we need is not necessarily an increase of faith. What we need is a faith that is pure. We need a heart from which all doubt has been purged, and according to the scripture in Psalm 8:2, the chatter of doubt is silenced by the weapon of praise: "You have ordained strength . . . That You may silence the enemy." It would seem impossible to doubt and to praise God at the same time. Praise is a high act of faith, and by continual praise we drive from our hearts the doubt that hinders our experience of God.

David, on another occasion during his wilderness wanderings, composed the sixty-third psalm, singing:

"Because Your lovingkindness is better than life, My lips
shall praise You. Thus I will bless You while I live; I will lift
up my hands in Your name . . . And my mouth shall praise
You with joyful lips . . . Because You have been my help,
Therefore in the shadow of Your wings I will rejoice."

—verses 3–5, 7

David vowed to joyfully praise the Lord "while I live." His offering of praise was a way of life rather than a part-time hobby.
In this Psalm he spoke of "those who seek my life, to destroy it"
(verse 9). But rather than murmuring with doubt, he rejoiced
with confidence, laying hold of God's power by feeding his
faith with joy.

Are there people aiming to destroy something valuable in
your life? Do the odds against you seem overwhelming and un-
fair? If so, remember that "The word of the LORD is proven" (Ps.
18:30), and His word to us is:

"Call upon Me in the day of trouble; I will deliver you, and
you shall glorify Me."

—Ps. 50:15

If the promise of God is that He will deliver us and we shall
glorify Him, then we should jump right out and get started by
glorifying Him with praise. "Whoever offers praise glorifies Me,"
and we should do this already, no matter what the circumstances
or the severity of the threat. Why should we wait to rejoice with
praise when we already have the assurance of God?

Another example of spiritual boldness is Paul's response to
"chains and tribulations" that awaited him. Meeting with the elders of the church in Ephesus, en route to Jerusalem where great
opposition had formed against him, he said:

"I go bound in the spirit to Jerusalem, not knowing the things that will happen to me there, except that the Holy Spirit testifies in every city, saying that chains and tribulations await me. But none of these things move me; nor do I count my life dear to myself, so that I may finish my race with joy."

—Acts 20:22–24a

In the long race for the prize of glory, our faith endures by feeding on joy. But where there is little joy, there is also little faith.

"All things are possible to him who believes" (Mark 9:23), and there is no greater show of faith than to concentrate on praising God in a situation beyond our strength and understanding. Praise is the weapon that God has ordained to silence the foe, and a believer should use this weapon relentlessly in all situations. When Paul and Silas were beaten and chained in prison, they relied on God through joyful praise in the name of Jesus:

"Then the multitude rose up together against [Paul and Silas]; and . . . when they had laid many stripes on them, they threw them into prison . . . and fastened their feet in the stocks. But at midnight Paul and Silas were praying and singing hymns to God, and the prisoners were listening to them. Suddenly there was a great earthquake, so that the foundations of the prison were shaken; and immediately all the doors were opened, and everyone's chains were loosed."

—Acts 16:22–26, brackets added

In your midnight hour, you too can seize the advantage with joyful songs of praise, crushing the doubt that would otherwise hinder "the power of God through faith" (1 Pet. 1:5). The shackles and chains oppressing you are not invulnerable; they cannot resist the power of God working through faith expressed in praise. When fear and doubt, depression or anxiety, rise in your heart, answer with joyful praise and stay on the offensive. Do not underestimate the biblical examples. Remember that David reached the throne of Israel after seventeen years of "hold[ing] fast the confidence and the rejoicing of the hope firm to the end" (Heb. 3:6).

# CHAPTER 3

# PRAISE HIM ALWAYS!

*"While I live, I will praise the LORD."*

—Ps. 146:2

## THE STORY

*After giving thanks to God for the denial, and for all He would accomplish for His glory through this painful turn of events, I focused my heart and mind on joyfully praising the Lord. During my twenty-six years in the faith, I felt that I had done my share of praising and giving thanks, but there was something different, something new and fresh, about this focused commitment to praise. For more than an hour, I did nothing except offer thanksgiving with adoration, feeling in my spirit a sweet enclosure of heavenly presence. Nothing had changed in my circumstances, but the hurtfulness that had pressed so hard against me seemed to have been pushed back, like an awful thing that still lurked near but could not reach in to touch me. I remembered and meditated on verses that I had memorized from the Book of Psalms, saying:*

"You are my hiding place . . . You shall surround me with songs of deliverance."

—32:7

"Oh, how great is Your goodness, Which You have laid up for those who fear You . . . You shall hide them in the secret place of Your presence."

—31:19–20

"In the secret place of His tabernacle He shall hide me; He shall set me high upon a rock."

—27:5

*Somewhere in all of that, I laid down and fell asleep.*

*When I woke up in the morning, the impulse to praise was still there. I came out of my cell at the unlock for the morning meal, and as the day went on, I held to the upper hand by fighting against every doubt, pain, and fear with the weapon of joyful praise. I kept reminding myself that, since all things are possible to those who believe, the greatest of all enemies is doubt, and it seemed the only way to truly drive out doubt was to steadily assault it with praise. With Christ in front of my eyes, I focused all of my heart, mind, soul, and strength on praising God through Him. I seized on the wisdom of Hebrews 13:15, which says, "By [Christ], let us CONTINUALLY offer the sacrifice of praise to God, that is, the fruit of our lips, giving thanks to His name" (emphasis mine). I connected this with Psalm 71:14, "But I will hope continually, and will praise You yet more and more." I rejoiced in this wisdom of determining that, no matter how much is coming* against me, I will hope in God continually and will praise Him more and more. I said to myself, 'There is no law against this . . . I am free to praise without limit . . . There is no boundary to how much I can use my mind to joyfully worship the Lord and thank Him forever!' I did not do this perfectly. I did not maintain an unbroken stride of triumph, but I kept stumbling forward with praise in my thoughts and on my lips.

As the days passed, I began noticing how the focused emphasis on praise led to a positive effect in my spiritual conversation with others, whether Christians or non-Christians. I could see the Spirit bringing me to a new reach of effectiveness in witness and ministry. Then, one night in my cell, I opened my Strong's Concordance and decided to begin an exhaustive study on what the Bible teaches about praise. Over the next few weeks, day and night, with every available hour, I stayed in my cell and carefully read every single verse in the Bible that uses words such as praise, joy, rejoicing, gladness, and thanksgiving. I began to see a powerful connection between the offering of praise and the walk of faith. Ephesians 5:18–20 spoke strongly to me about the link between walking in the Spirit and filling my heart with music to God. I also gave special attention to songs in the Book of Revelation, how the inhabitants of heaven are always praising God, and I connected this with the words of Jesus to the Father: "Your will be done on earth as it is in heaven." I knew that if this is what they are always doing in heaven, then this is what I should always be doing on earth.

After a few weeks of searching the Bible for an understanding of how joyful praise and thanksgiving work together with faith, I felt amazed, to say it lightly, at seeing example after example of God acting through the praise of His people in impossible situations. There was the story of Jehoshaphat and the army of Judah, in Second Chronicles chapter twenty, where they put singers in *front of the soldiers going out to battle, and when the worshipers began to sing and to praise, God went into action and seized the battle for Judah's favor. There was Paul and Silas, chained to a wall in the prison with bloody wounds on their backs, and at midnight they were praising God rather than doubting, fearing and complaining. I knew that in my own midnight hour I wanted to be found praising God, and I reasoned that if the Lord worked in this way through the praise of His people in their biblical lifetimes, why should He not work mightily through a determined outpouring of praise in my life? Romans 15:4 instructed me that "whatever things were written before, were written for our learning, that we through the patience and comfort of the scriptures might have hope." I also connected this teaching on praise with the story of Jacob clinging to God and refusing to let go (Gen. 32). I felt my spirit rising up fiercely in joyful excitement and saying to the Lord, "I will cling to You in praise and will not let go!"*

*As previously mentioned, I had been walking with the Lord Jesus in a serious way for three decades, with praise, joy, and thanksgiving being an important part of my spiritual life. But this new focus on praise was different, in terms of depth and magnitude. I felt I was climbing toward a new mountaintop of spiritual experience—not a mystical, imaginative experience, but one that came through the direct witness of scripture again and again and again, from Genesis through Revelation.*

*About two months after the denial, I put in front of me the accumulated pages of typewritten verses, many hundreds of scriptures on joy, praise, and thanksgiving, along with the many comments that I had written in spaces between the verses. I began to structure all of this into a series of studies.*

*One day at my workplace, I started sharing with my dear friend and Christian brother, Carlos Aceves, what I had been learning from God's word about the role of praise in the walk of faith. I shared with Carlos how this focus on praise was impacting me, how it was helping me grow in my experience of Christ and in my outlook on all things, including harshly difficult situations. After I had shared some of this, Carlos looked at me with a big smile and said, "This is revolutionary!" From that moment, he was right there with me in these studies on praise.*

*Every day at work, Carlos and I discussed these verses and examples from God's word. Then, I began to develop the studies into chapters for a book. This process went quickly, since I had been deeply immersed in the study of praise and had accumulated extensive lists of scriptures with comments. In less than two weeks, a draft of eight chapters was ready for polishing. Each day at our workplace, in an area where no one would disturb us, we gave time to reading and talking about the chapters. Carlos sat in a chair while I walked back and forth, reading aloud. He has a very strong gift for focused concentration, and he would close his eyes while I read. When I finished the chapter, he opened his eyes and began to comment. His ability for recall is truly amazing, and he would talk with me point by point through the chapter, bringing suggestions on where he felt the writing could be improved. Through his assistance, Christ enabled me to develop the original Bible Study sections of the chapters of this book.*

*From the outside, Fred Mendrin became very interested in this focus on praise, at a time when he was walking through the greatest trial of his life since he came into the faith. When I would speak with Fred on the phone or during a visit, we talked excitedly about God's will for us to joyfully praise Him continuously with thanksgiving in all situations. We talked about putting praise ahead of every concern, every decision, every thought—to put praise out in front of every battle the way that King Jehoshaphat put his singers in front of his soldiers. We took this very seriously, and we saw the difference it was making in our walk with Christ and our witness with others.*

*As I went about my days in the prison, there were still the daily emotional challenges. I mentioned in a previous chapter how for four months, since the attorney's assurance of a release through the courts, I enjoyed a delightful, tickly feeling in my soul. I had expected, based on the word of assurance from a man, to be out of prison within a year. Well, that was the word of a man. I had set myself up for a devastating disappointment by putting that much expectation on the word of assurance from a man. But now I had something different—the word of assurance from God. I did not know if I would ever be released from state prison, but I knew that by putting praise in front of everything, I could live a joyful life of triumphant fruitfulness for Christ's kingdom and glory beyond what I knew how to imagine. In that season of extreme adversity and material helplessness, I joyfully embraced the assurances of "Him who is able to do exceedingly abundantly above all I can ask or think" (Eph. 3:20).*

*There were times when I would momentarily sink back into frustration, feeling in my body and soul the weight of the years, the possibility that I would die of old age in state prison, or would someday receive a phone call saying my father was no longer around, or some other horrible news. I had been given a good life on this earth, and along with badly damaging the happiness and welfare of others, I had destroyed my own life while still a youth. But in those episodes of heaviness, the presence of Christ brought me back to what I was learning from scripture about praise, and I would rebound. Instead of waiting for an emotional change to come about with the passage of time, I produced an emotional change by an act of faith, recapturing the joy that is called in scripture "the joy of the Lord." Then, on the following day or soon thereafter, I would struggle again with the sharp pangs of fear and heaviness.*

*This is where the power of Christ through His body, the church, the fellowship of the saints, came in strong for me. When I shared with other Christians the recurring challenge of confusion about my life and uncertainty about my future, the brothers reminded me of what I had been teaching them about focusing totally on praise and thanksgiving. What a joy, to be wisely instructed by those one has taught! So, I was learning that, no matter how I might grow in the knowledge of God's word about the role of praise in the walk of faith, or in any other area of spiritual knowledge and development, I could only experience the full reality of it, the richness and power and wisdom of it, in the deep and daily fellowship of the Christians.*

*And the years passed . . .*

# BIBLE STUDY

Do you ever struggle with feelings of spiritual insignificance? This is a painful problem for many Christians who truly love the Lord but do not feel valuable to God's kingdom. There are Christians who routinely spend hours in self-indulgence through television or other non-edifying entertainments, not because their desire to serve Christ is lacking, but rather because they do not believe they can bring a meaningful contribution to the work of the kingdom. A remedy for spiritual discouragement is knowing the place of praise in everyday spiritual triumph.

\* \* \* \*

By offering praise, we declare that we are the people of God:

"This people I have formed for Myself, they shall declare My praise."

—Isa. 43:21

"But you [who come to God through Christ] are . . . His own special people, that you may proclaim the praises of Him who called you out of darkness into His marvelous light; who once were not a people but are now the people of God."

—1 Pet. 2:9–10a, brackets added

By proclaiming His praise, we position ourselves aggressively in the ministry of God's people, and by continuing in praise, the fruitfulness of our spiritual lives increases dramatically.

The following verses confirm the link between praise and increase:

"Let the people praise You, O God; Let all the peoples praise You. Then the earth shall yield her increase; God, our own God, shall bless us."

—Ps. 67:5–6

Is your life afflicted with scarcity? If so, start praising God and watch what happens. The scripture tells us "the desert shall rejoice and blossom as the rose" (Isa. 35:1b), and in this verse we note how the praise of rejoicing precedes the blossom. If your life feels like a desert, rejoice in Christ all day long, and your desert will sprout and blossom and spill over with fruit.

By abiding in joyful praise, we walk in the wisdom of those who triumph through the name of the Lord, but the unbelieving world grows ever more foolish through its refusal to glorify heaven's King with praise and thanksgiving:

For since the creation of the world . . . they are without excuse, because, although they knew God, they did not glorify [praise] Him as God, nor were thankful, but became futile in their thoughts, and their foolish hearts were darkened.

—Rom. 1:20–21, brackets added

Denying the Lord praise leads to futile thinking and darkness of heart. Denying Him praise identifies a person with the unbelieving world, but through a lifestyle of praise we set our minds on things above to embrace the customs of heaven.

Our Lord Jesus Christ prayed: "Our Father in heaven . . . Your will be done On earth as it is in heaven" (Matt. 6:9–10). In heaven, they are always praising God:

"And they do not rest day or night, saying: 'Holy, holy, holy, Lord God Almighty, Who was and is and is to come!'"

—Rev. 4:8b

If this is what they are always doing in heaven, this is what we should always be doing on earth. By praising God, we breathe the culture and the atmosphere of heaven, and we fulfill the scripture that tells us to "set your mind on things above, not on things on the earth" (Col. 3:2). In times of distress, we can lean on our own understanding and focus on the power of what rises against us, or we can walk on the stormy water by fixing our mind on Jesus with steadfast songs of praise.

The scripture in Isaiah tells us: "You will keep him in perfect peace, Whose mind is stayed on You" (26:3), and there is no better way to fix our minds on Jesus than to ceaselessly offer the sacrifice of praise.

The scripture tells us that God is "a rewarder of those who

diligently seek Him" (Heb 11:6), and "those who seek Him will praise the LORD" (Ps. 22:26). If we are not praising God, are we truly seeking Him? If we are truly seeking Him, we will not stop praising Him.

The scriptures repeatedly emphasize how those who seek the Lord must do so with constant and wholehearted praise:

> "Glory in His holy name; Let the hearts of those rejoice who seek the LORD."
>
> —1 Chron. 16:10

> "Let all those who seek You rejoice and be glad in You."
>
> —Ps. 40:16a

> "I will praise the LORD with my whole heart."
>
> —Ps. 111:1

> "I will bless the LORD at all times; His praise shall continually be in my mouth."
>
> —Ps. 34:1

> "I will sing to the LORD as long as I live; I will sing praise to my God while I have my being."
>
> —Ps. 104:33

> "Bless the LORD, O my soul; and all that is within me, bless His holy name!"
>
> —Ps. 103:1

> "Let my mouth be filled with Your praise And with Your glory all the day."
>
> —Ps. 71:8

When adversities storm against us, and the pain of helplessness overwhelms us, we show boldness of faith by saying with the psalmist:

"I will hope continually, And will praise You yet more and more. My mouth shall tell of Your righteousness And Your salvation all the day, For I do not know their limits."
—Ps. 71:14–15

By constantly praising God, we show a faith that sets no limits on what He will accomplish. As Gabriel said to the rejoicing virgin: "For with God nothing will be impossible" (Luke 1:37). If He can bring a child from a virgin who believed, why set a limit on what He will accomplish through the boldness of your joyful faith today? When the Israelites lifted their voice in praise to God, the walls of Jericho fell (Josh. 6:20), and "whatever things were written before were written for our learning" (Rom. 15:4). We learn from Jericho, and from other biblical examples, that "the weapons of our warfare are . . . mighty in God for pulling down strongholds" (2 Cor. 10:4). Whatever adversities and threats are coming against you, there is no opposition equal to the power of God working through faith expressed in joyful praise. No matter what your circumstances, you can say with Hannah the mother of Samuel, "I smile at my enemies, Because I rejoice in Your salvation" (1 Sam. 2:1).

By praising God you will lay hold of His strength: "The LORD is my strength and song" (Ps. 118:14). The apostle Paul constantly, at all times and in all situations, offered to God the sacrifice of praise through Jesus Christ, and because of this, he could boldly say: "I can do all things through Christ who strengthens me" (Phil. 4:13). As David in the wilderness also testified with joyful song: "For by You I can run against a troop, By my God I can leap over a wall" (Ps. 18:29).

If your life is afflicted by a wall of opposition, you can make a leap by shouting to God with joyful praise.

> "Oh, clap your hands, all you peoples! Shout to God with the voice of triumph!"
>
> —Ps. 47:1

> "Shout joyfully to the LORD, all the earth; Break forth in song, rejoice, and sing praises."
>
> —Ps. 98:4

If a troop of adversity comes against you, you can boldly say with the psalmist: "Though an army may encamp against me, My heart shall not fear; Though war may rise against me, In this I will be confident" (Ps. 27:3).

When the rebellious tribes of Israel came to fight against the house of David, which reigned over the kingdom of Judah, the army of Judah found itself caught in a pincer movement with no way to escape:

> "Jeroboam [king of the breakaway tribes of Israel] caused an ambush to go around behind them; so they were in front of Judah, and the ambush was behind them. And when Judah looked around, to their surprise the battle line was at both front and rear."
>
> —2 Chron. 13:13–14a, brackets added

Outmaneuvered by their opponents, and facing almost certain defeat, the men of Judah "cried out to the LORD, and the priests sounded the trumpets. Then the men of Judah gave a shout; and as the men of Judah shouted, it happened that God struck Jeroboam and all Israel . . . And the children of Israel fled before Judah, and God delivered them into their hand" (verses 14b–16).

Do you feel ambushed "at both the front and the rear"? Do you see opposition staring down from strong positions? Whatever your difficulties, or the strength of the odds against you, you too can "shout to God with the voice of triumph" and boldly rejoice in "the victory through our Lord Jesus Christ" (Ps. 47:1b; 1 Cor. 15:57).

By constant rejoicing in the name of Christ, all doubt is put to silence, so that "we may boldly say: 'The LORD is my Helper; I will not fear. What can man do to me?' " (Heb. 13:6).

By praising God we flee to His name. As the scripture says:

"Praise the LORD, call upon His name."

—Isa. 12:4

"According to Your name, O God, So is Your praise to the ends of the earth."

—Ps. 48:10

By praising His name, we walk in triumph: "To give thanks to Your holy name, To triumph in Your praise."

—Ps. 106:47b

By calling on Him with the voice of praise, we come to His name in truth. And, "the LORD is near to all who call upon Him, To all who call upon Him in truth" (Ps. 145:18).

When we offer praise, He fills our voice with the authority of His throne: "You are holy, Enthroned in the praises of Israel" (Ps. 22:3). All who come to God through Christ are authorized

to offer these praises: "Rejoice, O Gentiles, with His people . . .
Praise the LORD, all you Gentiles! Laud Him, all you peoples!"
(Deut. 32:43; Ps. 117:1). The great mystery of the Gospel is that
Christ has united all believers, regardless of race or nationality,
into one body of sonship:

"For you are all sons of God through faith in Christ Jesus . . .
that the Gentiles should be fellow heirs [with believing
Jews], of the same body, and partakers of His promise in
Christ through the gospel."
—Gal. 3:26; Eph. 3:6, brackets added

Through faith in Jesus we lift our voice with the praise in
which God sits enthroned. Knowing this, we should boldly seize
the word which tells us to "be filled with the Spirit, speaking to
one another in psalms and hymns and spiritual songs, singing
and making melody in your heart to the Lord" (Eph. 5:18b–19).
In these verses, we understand that by filling our hearts with
songs of praise, we have filled our hearts with the Spirit of God.

The scripture teaches us that the Lord acts through the praise
of His people:

"When I cry out to You, Then my enemies will turn back;
This I know, because God is for me. In God (I will praise
His word), in the LORD (I will praise His word), In God I
have put my trust."
—Ps. 56:9–11a

"God has gone up [He acts!] with a shout, The LORD with
the sound of a trumpet. Sing praises to God, sing praises!
Sing praises to our King, sing praises!"
—Ps. 47:5–6, brackets added

If you have no trumpet to blow, slap your hand on the table and shout to God in triumph! Acknowledge Him with joyful noises, remember the scripture which tells us, "Blessed are the people who know the joyful sound!" (Ps. 89:15a). Regardless of your circumstances or the threats to your success, show your confidence in the Lord by singing to Him with joy, knowing that those who commit their lives to praising God will not be denied the power of His favor.

We show our trust in the Father through Jesus by calling on Him with praise:

"I will call upon the LORD, who is worthy to be praised; So shall I be saved from my enemies."

—2 Sam. 22:4

The Book of Judges records for our learning how the Lord worked with power through the praise of His people when the homeland of Israel came under attack in the days of Gideon:

"Then all the Midianites and Amalekites, the people of the East, gathered together; and they crossed over and encamped in the Valley of Jezreel."

—6:33

The combined force of the enemy was too great for numbering:

"[They] were lying in the valley as numerous as locusts; and their camels were without number, as the sand by the seashore in multitude."

—7:12, brackets added

Gideon went up against this force with only three hundred of his men, and the outnumbered Israelites brought swords to the battle, but they did not rely on these:

> "Then [Gideon] divided the three hundred men into three companies, and he put a trumpet into every man's hands, with empty pitchers, and torches inside the pitchers . . . [they] came to the outpost of the camp at the beginning of the middle watch . . . Then the three companies blew the trumpets and broke the pitchers . . . and they cried, 'The sword of the LORD and of Gideon!' And every [Israelite] man stood in his place all around the camp; and the whole army ran and cried out and fled."
> —7:16, 19–20, brackets added

As in the days of Jehoshaphat, so also in the days of Gideon, when the people of God advanced with the weapon of praise, the enemies fell back in confusion:

> "When the three hundred blew their trumpets, the LORD set every man's sword against his companion throughout the whole camp; and the army fled."
> —Judg. 7:22a

The Lord delights to manifest His power through praise, and with such an abundance of biblical testimony, how can we justify doubt? As the scripture tells us in Isaiah: "If you will not believe, Surely you shall not be established" (7:9b). Even in the most complicated and difficult times, you can establish your authority as a royal priest in Christ by putting praise ahead of everything else you do.

The scripture in Ephesians tells us:

"Therefore, take up the whole armor of God, that you may be able to withstand in the evil day, and having done all, to stand."

—6:13

Only by constant praise can any of us say we have "done all." We do not put confidence in the praise itself, but rather in the power of God who works through faith expressed in praise. Nor should we think that praise is a magic formula; it is simply the wonderful means our God has ordained for us to experience His power for deliverance and triumph to the increase of His glory.

By proclaiming His praise, we declare that we are His people, and that we live always under "the favor You have toward Your people . . . the benefit of Your chosen ones" (Ps. 106:4–5).

Although our battles could seem to be against flesh and blood, the scriptures repeatedly assure us that "Heaven rules" (Dan. 4:26). By constantly praising God, we join the choir of heaven, and whatever comes against us comes also against the power and dominion of heaven's King.

By a lifestyle of praise, we bring to God through Christ a continual offering of sweet-smelling aroma, and by constantly praising God, we fill our hearts with His Spirit for an increase of fruitfulness and triumph in all situations.

Whatever confronts you in the present hour, whether it be fierce opposition outside of you or spiritual dryness inside of you, answer with praise and stay on the offensive, knowing from scripture that you can only be defeated when you stop praising God.

*started. If the assessment was High, they would have mentally decided against parole before I ever stepped into the room. So, one morning in early May, I was told to report to a certain area for my interview with the BPH psychologist. This is always an extremely high-pressure experience for an inmate, knowing that one wrongly-worded answer, or one inappropriate facial expression, can possibly be interpreted by the psychologist as reason for a push upward on the Risk Assessment. Going into the interview, I was excited about showing the psychologist documentation of my accomplishments in recent decades, the strength of my outside support, and how all of this change and positive development had resulted from my experience of Jesus Christ by faith.*

*The interview began well, with the psychologist noting the documentation of decades of good behavior and positive social involvement in the prisons. When he began asking questions about my insight into my criminal history and what I had done to work on the deep character defects that had led to such a horrible criminal past, I first expressed a deep shame and remorse for the damage and loss of life I had caused, and for the trouble I had brought to society. I then explained how the character defects such as hard-core rebelliousness and insensitivity to others connected, on one level, to low self-esteem and deep insecurities. So far, the psychologist was liking all of this, as I was telling him exactly what the inmates are trained in the "self-help" groups to say at these interviews and hearings. But his expression toward me began to change when I explained my understanding of myself on a deeper level.*

*I calmly stated that, in my understanding, issues like low self-esteem and personal insecurities are the result of a deeper, root cause of what the Bible calls "sin." I asserted that what led to my documented change of character and behavior starting in 1981 was not a gradual growth in understanding and addressing*

*issues like self-esteem, but rather a sudden experience of know-
ing that I am accountable to God for every word, thought, and
action, and that I have access to an entirely new identity by faith
in Jesus Christ. I told him that I will always want to continue growing as a person and to continue learning more about character
deficiencies and positive development, but that my change from
criminal to non-criminal personality came about in the moment
of spiritual rebirth accompanied by repentance and faith in the
Son of God.*

*The psychologist watched me with a stone-like facial expres-
sion as I explained that my experience of faith in Christ produced
in my mind a desire to please God above all other concerns. I
described how this faith teaches me that the meaning of life is
to please my Creator and to honor Him in all situations, and
that God is watching everything that goes on in my mind and
my conduct. I told him that, although I do not apply this faith
perfectly, the Gospel enables me to deal effectively with issues
like guilt, fear, anger, and despair. I stated, calmly but firmly, that
I do not believe that I could have experienced this documented
change in my character and lifestyle if I had taken any other approach than faith in Christ and belief in the truth and wisdom
and authority of the Bible. I expressed how this transforming
experience of faith and accountability to God is sobering without
being terrifying, and that it provides me with a mental anchor
and a moral compass.*

*I finished by mentioning that, since my 1981 experience of
faith in Christ, I have felt no need to intoxicate my brain with foreign substances, not only because the scripture assures me that I
cannot be influenced by God's Spirit while under the influence
of a foreign substance, but also because the beauty of knowing
Jesus Christ is so deeply satisfying that the deceptive attraction
of escape through drugs or alcohol is insulting to me. I told the*

doctor that, from beginning to end, the influence of Christ is responsible for any and all positive changes in my values, attitude, outlook, and lifestyle, and that if I were to ascribe credit to any other source, I would be lying.

Well, to put it lightly, the psychologist was visibly contemptuous of my answers. He wrote, on page ten of his report, that "Mr. Griffin's fervent religiosity could be interpreted as delusional." On page fourteen, he recommended to the BPH that I pose a "high risk" to commit a violent crime if released from prison. When I read those statements, which I knew would carry decisive weight at my parole hearing, I struggled deeply with feelings of humiliation, fear, and helplessness. But I also knew that I alone was responsible for putting my life in a situation where a person with authority could write about me anything that he chose.

On pages five and eleven of his report, the psychologist wrote that I lack insight into myself and into my history of alcohol abuse and criminality. On pages eleven and twelve, he wrote that I lack remorse and accountability for the harm I have caused to others. On page thirteen, he wrote that my personality shows "antisocial" features, and on page eight, he wrote that I am "odd." I felt that some of his statements were unprofessional, personally biased, and at times less than honest, and I began to struggle with anger. I knew that I needed to flee to the only refuge I know, the strong tower of the name of the Lord. I kneeled on the floor and poured out my soul in brokenness before Christ who opens what no one shuts, and shuts what no one opens (Rev. 3:7), and I confessed that, because of the awfulness of my criminal history, and the pain and loss that I have caused others to suffer, I do not deserve to even be considered for parole. But I also pleaded with the Lord that, for His name's sake, he would cause the panel to distinguish between who I was then and who I am now.

*I acknowledged that every horrible thing written about my crim-inal history is true, but the things written against who I am today are not true.*

*Several weeks later, when I sat in front of the panel, it was clear from the outset that their decision to deny parole had been made before the hearing even started. I was given what is called a "three-year denial," meaning I would need to wait three more years before my next parole hearing.*

*After leaving the large room where the hearing was held, I passed the small room where an attorney once assured me I would be out of prison within a year. Coming to the end of the hallway, I began walking down the cement staircase leading to the corridor. I reflected on how, in 2007, I had come down this staircase with the delightful expectation of release within a year, and now, three years later, I was on these same steps after receiv-ing a denial that would stretch out for another three years. The hardest part was going to the yard, getting in line for a phone call, and having a beloved family member accept the call with excitement and the expectation of hearing a good word, only to be told once again that I was denied parole. I do not remember which family member I spoke with, but I do remember feeling enormous pain, helplessness, and humiliation. I walked away from the phone with nothing left except my freedom to worship God and give thanks to Him that I was alive to live for His honor. Offering praise and thanksgiving did not drive out the heaviness, not at that time, but I knew that my only wisdom was to worship.*

*Soon after that call, the prison went on lockdown for the rest of the day. Dinner was brought to our cells that evening. In my mind, I believed this was the best thing for me. Rather than being out among the crowds and fellowshipping with other Christians, I felt it was good for me to be alone, to focus before the Lord on how I needed to think about all of this. After going into my cell, for the rest of the evening and the night, and each time I woke up during the night, I sang and offered prayers of thanksgiving, grateful that I could hope in the Lord and please Him by faith. But no matter how much I focused on worship, on filling my heart with thanksgiving and ceaseless prayer, the heaviness clung to me, and I did not understand why.*

*The next day we came off the short lockdown. I skipped the morning meal but later went to the yard and walked straight to the area where the Christians gather. As I fellowshipped with the brothers, enjoying spiritual communion with those who fear God and who love to talk of His kingdom and glory, I noticed the heaviness beginning to lift. Two hours later, at the midday voluntary recall, I decided to go in for lunch and come back out at the afternoon release. As I walked away from the area where the Christians gather, from about twenty yards behind me I heard the voice of Joseph, one of the elders in the faith, calling me. When I turned, he lifted his arm and reached high with a fist of triumph, and he said with a loud voice, "We will triumph in His praise!"*

*When Joseph shouted out in triumph, I felt in my spirit the force of life and wisdom in his words. Nothing in my life situation had changed, but having come out of my cell with a burden that would not go away, I now left the yard on a cloud of spiritual triumph. No matter how much I had praised the Lord in isolation, the heaviness would not leave until I stood in the fellowship of the saints.*

# BIBLE STUDY

Do you feel that your spiritual life is less fruitful than it should be? Having believed on Jesus as Christ and Lord, are you disappointed with your growth in godliness? Are you discouraged by the burden of so many problems?

If your current circumstances are troubling, or if your spiritual life seems dry and inconsistent, you can seize "the power of God through faith" (1 Pet. 1:5) by filling your heart with praise. By constant praise, you will enter into new opportunities for contributing to the work of the kingdom, and you will experience a refreshing increase of spiritual empowerment for fruitful labors and everyday godliness.

\* \* \* \*

The scripture links the meaning of life with praise, teaching us that our offerings to God are the true pleasure and value of being alive:

"Let my soul live, and it shall praise You."

—Ps. 119:175a

"Because Your lovingkindness is better than life, My lips shall praise You. Thus I will bless You while I live; I will lift up my hands in Your name."

—Ps. 63:3–4

Those of us pushing up in years are sometimes amazed at how quickly a lifetime can pass. Seasons of happiness delight us while they last, and we do our best to relish the beauty of each moment, but the moment slips away and never comes back. Poets speak often of "the days of the lost sunshine," and the scripture also refers to how quickly "the grass withers, the flower fades" (Isa. 40:8). The earth spins, and we all know the yearning for good things lost to the curse of time, but, through Jesus our Lord, we have power to "redeem the time" and possess each moment forever:

"The grass withers, the flower fades, But the word of our God stands forever."

—Isa. 40:8

If the word of the Lord stands forever, then by all means we should invest every moment in the word. And the word of the Lord tells us:

"Whoever offers praise glorifies Me."

—Ps. 50:23a

Time that is used for self-indulgence is lost to the past and cannot be retrieved, but a moment invested in the Father's glory is a moment that lives forever in the kingdom of God. It is a moment stored up "in heaven, where neither moth nor rust destroys and where thieves do not break in and steal" (Matt. 6:20). When the Lord extended Hezekiah's life, the king measured the value of his years by the opportunity those years would provide for bringing glory to God:

"For Sheol cannot thank You, Death cannot praise You . . . The living, the living man, he shall praise You As I do this day."

—Isa. 38:18–19a

As citizens of the kingdom, we measure life's value by the opportunity it provides for bringing glory to God, and we can glorify Him with praise at all times in all situations:

"While I live I will praise the LORD; I will sing praises to my God while I have my being."

—Ps. 146:2

"Therefore by [Christ] let us continually offer the sacrifice of praise to God, that is, the fruit of our lips, giving thanks to His name."

—Heb. 13:15

We should praise the Father through Jesus—not sometimes, and not most of the time. We should praise the Lord as often as we breathe. For those who come to God through Christ, joyful praise is spiritual breathing. "Let everything that has breath praise the LORD" (Ps. 150:6). But when we are not praising God, we are spiritually suffocating.

Jesus explained: "By this My Father is glorified, that you bear much fruit" (John 15:8). This compares with: "Whoever offers praise glorifies Me" (Ps. 50:23). Every moment of life is opportunity to glorify God with the fruit of praise, "speaking to one another in psalms and hymns and spiritual songs, singing and making melody in your heart to the Lord, giving thanks always for all things to God the Father in the name of the Lord Jesus Christ" (Eph. 5:19–20).

We should praise Him with our deeds, our words, our thoughts, and we should use the imagination of our hearts to devise new ways of joyfully praising Him. By a lifestyle of praise, we lay hold of the fullness that our Lord came to give, and the spiritual value of praise could not possibly be overestimated.

As a general rule, and whenever possible, what should the people of God be talking about?

"They shall speak of the glory of Your kingdom, And talk of Your power."

—Ps. 145:11

"Sing to Him, sing psalms to Him; Talk of all His wondrous works! Glory in His holy name."

—Ps. 105:2–3a

If you seriously desire a more fruitful spiritual life, spend as much time as possible with people who habitually celebrate the kingdom of God in their conversations. The scripture tells us that the Lord listens with delight to the conversation of those who speak to one another of His goodness and glory:

"Then those who feared the LORD spoke to one another, And the LORD listened and heard them; So a book of remembrance was written before Him For those who fear the LORD And who meditate on His name."

—Mal. 3:16

We should not underestimate the compromising effect of worldly conversation. This is a terrible plague that weakens the faith of many believers, and whatever weakens faith also weakens our experience of the Lord's power in our lives. Worldly conversation is not necessarily vulgar, but it does not edify, and whatever does not edify is of no value to God's kingdom or to His glory among men.

The power and wisdom of godly conversation is emphasized throughout scripture, and we are told that "whatever you do in word or deed, do all in the name of the Lord Jesus" (Col. 3:17). The entire stream of our conversation should be an offering to God through Christ, as Paul tells us again in Colossians:

"Let your speech always be with grace, seasoned with salt .
. . teaching and admonishing one another in psalms and
hymns and spiritual songs."

—4:6; 3:16

The scripture speaks of "redeeming the time" (Col. 4:5), and
we should be jealous for the Lord's glory with every moment.

If we are serious in our aim to more richly express the fullness of life that Christ came to give, we will fill our hearts with
constant praise that spills over in the general flow of our speech.

"I will also meditate on all Your work, And talk of Your deeds."

—Ps. 77:12

"My mouth shall tell of Your righteousness And Your
salvation all the day . . . Let my mouth be filled with Your
praise And with Your glory all the day . . . My tongue also
shall talk of Your righteousness all the day long."

—Ps. 71:15, 8, 24

By filling your heart with constant praise, you will quickly notice that worldly conversation has lost its appeal. By filling your
heart with constant praise, you will also notice a newfound joy
and confidence in speaking with others about the kingdom of
God. And by filling your heart with constant praise, you will notice the power of God taking control of your life.

According to scripture, the truly "good life," the "beautiful
life," is a life of constantly praising God:

"Praise the LORD! For it is good to sing praises to our God;
For it is pleasant, and praise is beautiful."

—Ps. 147:1

"It is good to give thanks to the LORD, And to sing praises to Your name, O Most High."

—Ps. 92:1

"Rejoice in the LORD, O you righteous! For praise from the upright is beautiful."

—Ps. 33:1

Wherever you are, whatever the situation, you can live the good life by praising God continuously with joyful song. Every human is obligated to live for God's praise (Ps. 150:6). And those who rejoice in this obligation identify themselves as "the people of God":

"But you are a chosen generation . . . His own special people, that [so that, in order that] you may proclaim the praises of Him who called you out of darkness into His marvelous light; who once were not a people, but are now the people of God."

—1 Pet. 2:9–10a, brackets added

When the Lord tells us, "Whoever offers praise glorifies Me" (Ps. 50:23), He shows us how to abide in what is most precious to Him. For those who truly love God, the highest experience of happiness is the joy of pleasing the Father through Christ, and we can do this continually by the sacrifice of praise to His name:

"Sing praises to His name, for it is pleasant."

—Ps. 135:3b

"I will praise the name of God with a song, And will magnify Him with thanksgiving. This also shall please the LORD."
—Ps. 69:30–31a

The true lovers of God testify openly:

"In God we boast all day long, And praise Your name forever."
—Ps. 44:8

Are you facing great opposition from external circumstances, or from struggles in your own heart? Start boasting in God all day long and watch what happens. Strongholds of opposition, both outside of you and within you, will come down by the power of God working through faith expressed in praise.

When we speak of praise we are speaking of faith. Praise is simply a bold expression of faith, and help is promised in time of need to those who come boldly:

"Let us therefore come boldly to the throne of grace, that we may obtain mercy and find grace to help in time of need."
—Heb. 4:16

"Christ Jesus our Lord, in whom we have boldness and access with confidence through faith in Him."
—Eph. 3:11b–12

There is a faith that merely believes, but the faith that moves mountains is the faith that shouts aloud with joyful praise and refuses to stop.

From Genesis through Revelation, the scripture charges us to express our love and faith toward God with joyful praises. The more aggressively we rejoice, the more richly we enter God's power working through faith. Since Christ is our King, and since there is no law against rejoicing, we should awake in the morning to "break forth in song" and "praise Him according to His excellent greatness!" (Ps. 98:4; 150:2).

The scripture in Isaiah speaks of "those who rejoice in My exaltation" (13:3). And if we have nothing else to do, we can joyfully thank the Lord for being alive to sing His praise.

The scripture records that when Solomon became king "they blew the horn, and all the people said, 'Long live King Solomon!' And all the people went up after him; and the people played the flutes and rejoiced with great joy, so that the earth seemed to split with their sound" (1 Kings 1:39–40). If they rejoiced like this at the rise of Solomon, how much more should we rejoice at the exaltation of Jesus who said, "A greater than Solomon is here" (Matt. 12:42)?!

Again, if the people rejoiced with such aggression that "the earth seemed to split" when they "went up after Solomon," how much more should we split the earth and the skies and the seas as we joyfully run after Jesus?

The Lord has promised deliverance to those who cling to Him in love:

"Because he has set his love upon Me, therefore I will deliver him."

—Ps. 91:14

There is no better way to focus our love on Christ than to joyfully praise His name. "Let those also who love Your name Be joyful in You" (Ps. 5:11b). By clinging to Christ in praise, we show that our love is set upon Him, and by this we see once again the connection between walking in praise and living in triumph.

We have seen how the Bible provides powerful examples of the Lord's people triumphing through praise against impossible odds. If your life is assaulted by problems beyond your strength and understanding, remember the examples of Jehoshaphat and Gideon and David and Paul and Silas. Without leaving other things undone, dare to put joyful praise ahead of every care, every effort, and every thought.

The scripture in James warns that "a double-minded man" is "unstable in all his ways," and "let not that man suppose that he will receive anything from the Lord" (1:7–8). The fullness of the blessing goes to those who live with single-minded commitment to God's glory in Christ, and for Christians who struggle with double-mindedness, there is nothing like praise to focus the mind on Jesus alone.

By receiving the baptism into our Lord Jesus Christ, we have taken a vow to war as soldiers against all that opposes the Father's glory in the Son. As Paul says to us all through Timothy:

> "You therefore must endure hardship as a good soldier of Jesus Christ. No one engaged in warfare entangles himself with the affairs of this life, that he may please him who enlisted him as a soldier."
>
> —2 Tim. 2:3–4

By continuously praising God, we leave no room in our hearts for entanglement with "the affairs of this life."

Our Lord warned of those "who hear the word, and the cares of this world, the deceitfulness of riches, and the desires for other things, entering in, choke the word, and it becomes unfruitful" (Mark 4:18b–19). For all who struggle with the entanglements of double-mindedness, the remedy is praise. By constantly praising God, a person becomes unable to mentally tolerate compromise, and constant praise will focus the mind for "bringing every thought into captivity to the obedience of Christ" (2 Cor. 10:5).

By diligent praise, we uphold "the shield of faith with which you will be able to quench all the fiery darts of the wicked one" (Eph. 6:16), and the scripture also tells us in Proverbs:

> "Keep your heart with all diligence, For out of it spring the issues of life."
>
> —4:23

By constant praise we maintain a steadfast heart, as David testified when he "fled from Saul into the cave" (Ps. 57:1):

> "My heart is steadfast, O God, my heart is steadfast; I will sing and give praise."
>
> —Ps. 57:7

Hiding in the cave like a cornered animal, David offered praise to keep his heart steady on God, and this provides yet another example of the power at work in our lives when we cling to God in praise.

Do you desire a more complete and richly satisfying experience of salvation? Once again, the gateway to fullness is praise:

> "But you shall call your walls Salvation, And your gates Praise."
>
> —Isa. 60:18b

By entering the gates of praise, we come to the walls of salvation. Knowing this, we should gladly say with the psalmist, "I will hope continually, And will praise You yet more and more" (Ps. 71:14). At all times and in all situations, the scripture tells us to "make the voice of His praise to be heard" (Ps. 66:8). And this is the wisdom of those who triumph through the name of the Lord.

The scripture speaks of "the exceeding greatness of His power toward us who believe" (Eph. 1:19). We are not told that God's power is great toward those who doubt. The fullness of life in Christ Jesus, with the "exceedingly great and precious promises" (2 Pet. 1:4), goes to those who "have faith and do not doubt" (Matt. 21:21). By filling our hearts with praise, we grow strong in the faith that crushes doubt for a life of triumph in Christ Jesus our Lord.

Is your life afflicted with scarcity? Are you helpless and in need? The scripture tells us in Psalms: "Let the poor and the needy praise Your name" (74:21). In your time of scarcity, give glory to God with the boldness of praise, and "the Father of mercies . . . shall supply all your needs according to His riches in glory by Christ Jesus" (2 Cor. 1:3; Phil. 4:19).

Without leaving other things undone, boldly put praise ahead of every effort and every thought. Are you unemployed and in need of a job? Hit the pavement with steps of praise, and God will direct your path to the greenest pasture. Do you lack confidence when being interviewed for a job? Fill your heart with joyful song all through the interview, and God will seize control. As David sang, "when he was in the wilderness of Judah" (Ps. 63:1) and greatly in need of help:

> "Because You have been my help, Therefore in the shadow
> of Your wings I will rejoice."
> —Ps. 63:7

Wherever you are, however great the need and however helpless and overwhelmed you feel, fill your heart with melody to the

Lord, rejoicing "in the shadow of Your wings," knowing that God has promised "help in time of need" to those who come boldly. And, "Has He said, and will He not do? Or has He spoken, and will He not make it good?" (Num. 23:19)

# CHAPTER 5

# GIVE THANKS ALWAYS!

*"In everything give thanks; for this is the will of God in Christ Jesus for you."*

—1 Thess. 5:18

## THE STORY

*Two more years passed since my fifth parole denial. A lot had been going on with ministry in the prison and with support on the outside. The former prison director, Jim Rowland, promised to write a letter of support for my next hearing, recommending to the BPH that I be released. Also, my sister, Pam, had invested in forming a company for the purpose of publishing and marketing my books. We decided to name the company in honor of our mother, calling it The Mary Ellen Group. Meanwhile, Fred had raised another $15,000 to pay the same attorney who filed the writ in 2007, and who now assured us an appeal of that denial stood a good chance of being overturned by a higher court. Also during those years, the ministry in the prison was bearing much* *fruit, with some of the younger Christians being raised into po-sitions of spiritual leadership that would provide experience to prepare them for a lifetime of godly service after release. I was excited about a lot of things, both on the inside and the outside.*

*The Lord had rescued me at age twenty-three from death and damnation, and had shepherded me on a new path through fire and water, decade after decade. Now, having reached my mid-fif-ties, I clung to the one thing which no one and nothing could take away, the freedom to live joyously for the honor of Christ and to trust that my times are truly in His hand.*

*In 2012, three developments came in rapid succession over a two-month period. In February, my birth mother, Martha, who did not raise me or have much to do with my upbringing from an early age, but whom I loved and regarded with the respect of a son toward a mother, slipped in the shower and suffered a head injury that left her in a coma. Five days later, she died.*

*Pam flew back east to the state where Mother lay in inten-sive care on life support. She was nearly brain dead and all her vital organs were shutting down, but from the yard in Soledad I spoke into her ear through the cell phone in Pam's loving hand. I acted in faith, defying the medical fact of Mother's comatose state, trusting the Holy Spirit to put my words into her spirit. I poured out my heart in loving gratefulness, thanking her for all the months she had carried me inside of her and for the early years when she nursed me as a baby. I told her that I was sorry for disappointing her so badly by turning to rebellion and crime in my teenage years, and for hurting so many others and spending so much of my life in jails and prisons. I knew that my mother was not saved, that she knew about God but had never placed her faith for salvation in Jesus Christ, so I said to her something like, "Mother, I want to see you again. I want you to be with us in a new body on a new earth forever. It is not too late. Mother, I urge you, right now, flee to Jesus the Son of God for your covering when you leave this world and face the judgment seat of God."*

*Although Mother could not talk or move, Pam told me that as I spoke into her ear, a tear formed in her left eye. Beyond that, I do not know anything with certainty. I only know that God enabled me, through my sister standing at Mother's bedside, to pour into her ear the testimony of Jesus as she was leaving this world.*

*After the call, I walked away from the phone with two of the Christians, one on each side. We walked in silence. With tears on my face and my mind in another place, the brothers escorted me around that large track. What a precious memory I have of those two Christians walking with me in a season like that, each of them showing the wisdom to know it was not a time to talk, but just to be there.*

*Less than two months after Mother's passing, I was told the U.S. 5th Circuit Court of Appeals had ruled against my appeal of the lower court's denial of the 2007 writ. For all of the early hope and assurance, and the cost for attorney fees, the effort to get me out of prison through the courts had failed. In that same week, Pam decided there was no wisdom in maintaining the cost of keeping the Mary Ellen Group viable with me in prison. We believed the books I had written were edifying and marketable, but without me physically present to speak in public and do the things an author must do for success in marketing, this investment with the Mary Ellen Group was not going to bear fruit. So, a week after the effort in the courts went down in defeat, and less than two months after Mother's burial, the dream of the Mary Ellen Group also fell into the grave. There was not much to be encouraged by, not in the visible world, but it was a time to remind myself of what I knew and believed at the deepest level. I thanked* the Lord for this opportunity to please Him with worship while the heaviness of grief was pulling so powerfully inside of me.

Another year passed, and I clung to Christ as my redemption and as the meaning and goal of my life. At the risk of sounding repetitious, I want to emphasize that I had my moments of doubt and struggle. Never doubting the truth of God's word or His power and wisdom, but at times really wondering if the Lord had a purpose for me beyond the prison walls. I hungered and thirsted for opportunity to show the outside world what Christ had done for me, but now that my twenties had passed, and then my thirties, and then my forties, and now half of my fifties, with no end in sight, I had my moments of doubt. Beginning one day in March of 2013, all of that began to change.

On that day I was walking the yard with one of the brothers, and I saw a Christian named Stefan calling to me from the phone area. I stepped off the track and approached Stefan, who handed me the receiver and said, "Hey, my friend Donnalee has a question about the Bible, do you think you could help her?" I took the receiver and spoke for the first time with Donnalee, a Christian lady who lived in Salt Lake City. She had a question about a situation in her life, and she needed an answer from the scriptures. Through my years and decades of reading, absorbing, living, and teaching God's word, when this moment of unexpected opportunity arrived, I was ready. The Lord had prepared me, and I took Donnalee to some verses in the Book of Ezekiel where her question was answered. We spoke for no more than three minutes, but the Holy Spirit was busy.

Donnalee and I began corresponding, and on December 28 of that year, she made the drive from Utah to Soledad, a thousand miles each way, to visit me. For more than six hours we sat at a table with an open Bible, talking about the beauty of Christ and the joy of knowing Him as our Shepherd, Savior, and Lord. We *spoke of some of our challenges and struggles, and how always, no matter what difficulties came upon us, Jesus Christ remained our assurance and our rest. At one point, which I recall with vivid distinction, Donnalee, holding an open Bible in her hands, looked up toward the lights and said something like, "I just want my life to always be on the altar for Christ." As I watched her, intently, I felt a deep fascination, like I was seeing a woman step out of the Bible. I knew that she absolutely meant what she had just said, and I saw her as one of those women in Hebrews chapter eleven, "of whom the world was not worthy" (verse 38). And I knew that God had raised up Donnalee to be my wife.*

*I had no income, no property, no physical impressiveness, and no assurance that I would ever be released from state prison. BUT GOD, who gives life to the dead, and who calls those things that do not exist as though they did (Rom. 4:17), HE had put into this woman's heart the certainty that I was the husband He had chosen in Christ for her. Staring at her lovely face as she expressed her adoration and passion for Christ, I felt the amazement of a man who is seeing the heavens opened and a gift from God descending, a gift more wonderful than I could ever have known how to imagine.*

*Eight months later, Donnalee had wrapped up her affairs in Utah, and on August 16 she made the long drive to relocate in the small city of Soledad. On that evening, a Friday, I went to the yard and called. She answered, and as I watched the sun setting behind the hills heading out toward Monterey, I listened to her delightful voice, telling me excitedly, "Honey, I'm about thirty miles from Soledad!" She had just passed through Salinas, on her way to a town where she did not know a soul. She would need to start everything from scratch. A job, a place to live, a church, new friends. She had left behind everything she knew of this world, to follow her Lord Jesus Christ and be as close as possible to the husband God had chosen to love her as Christ loves His church. As I stood at the phone and stared out toward the sunset, in my amazement, all I could think to say was, "I thank You and praise You, Lord God of mercy." At age twenty-three, God had snatched me from death while I held a noose in my hands. He had covered me with forgiveness and given me a heart to love and follow Him. Now, so many years later, He had brought to me a wife who so richly delights my soul that I fail to find words to adequately express my joy and gratitude!*

*Beginning in August of 2014, weekend after weekend, through summer, fall, winter, and spring, Donnalee was there on each visiting day. She would greet me with a hug and a kiss, use her hard-earned money to buy us meals and snacks, and hold my hand all through the day while we sat as close as the rules allowed. During those hours together, we shared with one another the dreams, fears, passions, and cares in our hearts, pouring out our souls in oneness as we prayed in the name of Christ that God would someday grant us a life together beyond the prison walls. At a certain place in that crowded, noisy room, we would sometimes stand by the bars, looking out through a sally port that led to an open door, through which we could see a tiny section of the outside world and the side of a large hill. As we stood by those bars, we spoke before the Lord of our dream to someday walk together out in that wide open, to have our own place to live, to walk trails and climb hills and feel on our backs the sunshine, and at night to look up at His stars in wonder and worship.*

*During those times in that visiting room, all we had was faith, hope, and love, and four years would pass before the Lord brought about a dramatic change in our situation. I will let my beloved wife tell that part of our story in later chapters, but I want to testify before Christ and God, and before men and angels, that Donnalee is to me the bursting of sunshine through a dark layer* of clouds, filling the valley of my life with the beauty and warmth of Christ's presence in a way that I had never before imagined.

I want to close my story in this book by saying that "when I am weak, then I am strong" (2 Cor. 12:10), that God "is able to do exceedingly abundantly above all that we ask or think" (Eph. 3:20), and that we can only be defeated when we stop praising God.

## BIBLE STUDY

Do your prayers seem weak and of little avail? If so, be encouraged to know the offering of thanks is scripturally guaranteed to ignite your faith and fill your heart with the joy of pleasing God. The following study shows from scripture how the continual giving of thanks will revolutionize your life and bring you deep into the fullness of God's promises in Christ.

\* \* \* \*

The Lord "is rich to all who call upon Him" (Rom. 10:12), and the proper way to call on Him is with the voice of thanksgiving:

"I will offer to You the sacrifice of thanksgiving, And will call upon the name of the LORD."

—Ps. 116:17

The scripture records how in a time of great danger, the prophet Daniel "prayed and gave thanks before his God, as was his custom since early days" (Dan. 6:10), and on that same day Daniel was thrown into a den of lions, where "no injury whatever was found on him, because he believed in his God" (Dan. 6:23). As a believer who relied on the Lord's favor in all situations,

Daniel's custom was to lace his prayers with thanksgiving, show-ing us by example how we can bring to our hearts the fire of conviction when we pray.

When Jonah rebelled and was brought down under severe punishment, he prayed from "the fish's belly" and said, "I will sac-rifice to You With the voice of thanksgiving" (Jon. 2:9). As with Daniel, the prophet Jonah offered his prayer with thanksgiving, and the following verse records the Lord's response:

> "So the LORD spoke to the fish, and it vomited Jonah onto dry land."
>
> —2:10

Whether we feel like Daniel, who had done nothing wrong but found himself in a den of lions, or like Jonah, who had done something wrong and found himself in the belly of a fish, we should learn from the prophets and call on the Lord "with the voice of thanksgiving" (Jon. 2:9). These biblical examples show how expressions of gratitude accompany the faith by which all things are possible.

The scriptures repeatedly emphasize the value of joyful thanksgiving in our approach to God:

> "Let us come before His presence with thanksgiving; Let us shout joyfully to Him with psalms."
>
> —Ps. 95:2

> "Enter into His gates with thanksgiving, And into His courts with praise. Be thankful to Him, and bless His name."
>
> —Ps. 100:4

As the people of God, we express our identity by a continual offering of good works and praise (Titus 2:14; Eph. 2:10; 1 Pet. 2:9). The giving of thanks relates closely to praise, and the two are often referred to interchangeably:

"I will give You thanks in the great assembly; I will praise You among many people."

—Ps. 35:18

"Sing to the LORD with thanksgiving; Sing praises on the harp to our God."

—Ps. 147:7

The praise of thanksgiving expresses our righteousness in Christ:

"Surely the righteous shall give thanks to Your name."

—Ps. 140:13a

As the people of God, redeemed in righteousness by the blood of the Son, every mention or remembrance of the Lord's name should cause the voice of thanksgiving to rise in our hearts:

"Sing praise to the LORD, you saints of His, And give thanks at the remembrance of His holy name."

—Ps. 30:4

By giving thanks to His name, we walk in the triumph of praise:

"To give thanks to Your holy name, To triumph in Your praise."

—Ps. 106:47

Joyful thanksgiving pours fuel on our spiritual flame to burn away doubt that hinders "the power of God through faith." When Jonah had no strength or wisdom for overcoming his impossible situation, he prayed with the voice of thanksgiving and triumphed through the power of God. This was "written for our learning" (Rom. 15:4), and, by the authority of biblical example, we learn that deliverance and triumph are certain for those who commit their lives to praising God with the voice of thanksgiving.

The apostle Paul explains that everything we say and do is to be an offering through Christ, but he emphasized that whatever we offer must be accompanied by thanksgiving:

"And whatever you do in word or deed, do all in the name of the Lord Jesus, giving thanks to God the Father through Him."

—Col. 3:17

Only by giving thanks is our offering of word and deed enriched by the name of Jesus.

The epistle of James assures us that "the effective, fervent prayer of a righteous man avails much" (5:16), but, by comparing scripture with scripture, we learn that "fervent prayer" is effective only when offered with thanks. As Paul tells us again in Colossians:

"Continue earnestly in prayer, being vigilant in it with thanksgiving."

—4:2

He writes of this again in Philippians, emphasizing how the

full involvement of God for deliverance and triumph becomes our experience only when prayer is offered with thanksgiving:

> "Be anxious for nothing, but in everything by prayer and supplication, with thanksgiving, let your requests be made known to God; and the peace of God, which surpasses all understanding, will guard your hearts and minds through Christ Jesus."
>
> —4:6–7

When we are helpless and without strength to change a situation, the prayer of aggressive thanksgiving drives out anxiety and brings to our hearts an outpouring of joyful peace that surpasses understanding. This is not the peace of an ostrich sticking its head in the sand to ignore the threatening issues; rather, it is the peace of knowing that God has seized control over our situation and is accomplishing the good that we ourselves could not hope to accomplish.

The apostle Paul gave enormous emphasis to thanksgiving in relation to prayer and to the whole of Christian living. The following is a brief sampling from his epistles, and we urge attention to the link between effective prayer and the giving of thanks:

> To the Christians in Rome: "First, I thank my God through Jesus Christ for you all"
>
> —Rom. 1:8.

> To those in Corinth: "I thank my God always concerning you"
>
> —1 Cor. 1:4.

To those in Ephesus: "I . . . do not cease to give thanks for you, making mention of you in my prayers"

—Eph. 1:15–16.

To those in Philippi: "I thank my God upon every remembrance of you, always in every prayer of mine making request for you all with joy"

—Phil. 1:3–4.

To those in Colossae: "We give thanks to the God and Father of our Lord Jesus Christ, praying always for you"

—Col. 1:3.

To those in Thessalonica: "We give thanks to God always for you all, making mention of you in our prayers" (1 Thess. 1:2). "For this reason we also thank God without ceasing" (1 Thess. 2:13). "We are bound to thank God always for you, brethren"

—2 Thess. 1:3.

To Timothy: "I exhort first of all that supplications, prayers, intercessions, and giving of thanks be made for all men" (1 Tim. 2:1). "I thank my God . . . as without ceasing I remember you in my prayers night and day"

—2 Tim. 1:3.

To Philemon: "I thank my God, making mention of you always in my prayers"

—Philem. 4.

The Bible consistently links thanksgiving with the power of God's working through prayer. Joyful thanksgiving is a show of boldness, expressing to God our confidence in His promise to act. If heartfelt expressions of gratitude have been lacking in your prayers, you will experience your own spiritual revival by committing your heart and tongue to a consistent outpouring of thanks.

A failure to be thankful, even in extreme adversity, places a person outside the will of God:

"In everything give thanks; for THIS is the will of God in Christ Jesus for you."

—1 Thess. 5:18, emphasis added

In telling us to give thanks in all things, Paul shows that continual thanksgiving brings everything that concerns us into the hand of God, and only by giving thanks do we keep ourselves in His will for the guarantee of His favor. But the person who withholds thanksgiving shows unbelief, and "let not that man suppose that he will receive anything from the Lord" (James 1:7).

The giving of thanks is described in scripture as a spiritual sacrifice to be offered with joy:

"Let them sacrifice the sacrifices of thanksgiving, And declare His works with rejoicing."

—Ps. 107:22

By constantly praising God with joyful thanksgiving, we also fill our hearts with light to walk in the confidence of His leading:

"Blessed are the people who know the joyful sound! They walk, O LORD, in the light of Your countenance. In Your name they rejoice all day long."

—Ps. 89:15–16a

Does your life seem so complicated that you "don't know what to do?" The wisdom of scripture instructs you to rejoice all day while offering thanks for the promise that His countenance will shine on your path.

> "In all your ways acknowledge Him, And He shall direct
> your paths."
> —Prov. 3:6

There is no better way to acknowledge Him than to joyfully thank Him for the promise. In the offering of praise we have made the acknowledgment, but when praise is withheld, there is no acknowledgment and we forfeit the guarantee.

When you are faced with a decision, whether big or small, rejoice with thanksgiving for the Lord's promise to fill your heart with wisdom and to "lead you in the paths of righteousness for His name's sake."

The scripture condemns the world for refusing to offer the praise of thanksgiving, saying in Romans that "they are without excuse, because, although they knew God, they did not glorify Him as God, nor were thankful, but became futile in their thoughts, and their foolish hearts were darkened" (1:20–21). Ingratitude is a fruit of unbelief and leads to further mental decay. In contrast, by continually thanking God we fill our hearts with light that leads to sound thinking in all things.

Under the old covenant, with its great emphasis on animal sacrifice, the offering of thanks was more pleasing to God than the sacrifice of bulls and goats:

"I will praise the name of God with song, And will magnify Him with thanksgiving. This also shall please the LORD better than an ox or bull."

—Ps. 69:30–31

As the sheep of Christ, we are able to please and magnify God at all times with the voice of thanksgiving:

"So we, Your people and sheep of Your pasture, Will give You thanks forever."

—Ps. 79:13

Every moment of wakefulness provides opportunity to magnify God with the praise of thanksgiving:

"At midnight I will rise to give thanks to You."

—Ps. 119:62a

As believers in the goodness of God, thanksgiving should be the atmosphere of our thoughts and conversation, "singing and making melody in your heart to the Lord, giving thanks always for all things to God the Father in the name of our Lord Jesus Christ" (Eph. 5:19–20). Thanksgiving should saturate our speech and characterize our lifestyle, as Paul says again when he exhorts us to not indulge in "foolish talking, nor coarse jesting, which are not fitting, but rather giving of thanks" (Eph. 5:4).

By offering thanks, we express our confidence that God is good:

"Oh, give thanks to the LORD, for He is good!"

—Ps. 106:1a

For those who love Christ, the great value of living is the

opportunity to glorify God and to please Him continually with songs of gratitude and works of faith. This is the truly godly life:

> "It is good to give thanks to the LORD, And to sing praises to Your name."
>
> —Ps. 92:1

The psalmist asks to be delivered from death in order to continue giving thanks:

> "For in death there is no remembrance of You; In the grave who will give You thanks?"
>
> —Ps. 6:5

Wherever we are, in whatever situation, we can live the good life by praising God with songs of thanksgiving. As Paul, who gave thanks "without ceasing," testified in a letter written from jail: "I have learned in whatever state I am, to be content" (Phil. 4:11). As Christians, we are able to invest every moment with eternal value by filling the moment with the praise of thanksgiving.

By the continual giving of thanks, our faith takes wings and all things become possible. When Jesus gave thanks for the seven loaves, the power of God multiplied the food for feeding a multitude:

> "And He took the seven loaves and the fish and gave thanks, broke them and gave them to His disciples; and the disciples gave to the multitude. So they all ate and were filled."
>
> —Matt. 15:36–37a

The scripture in John refers to this as "the place where they ate bread after the Lord had given thanks" (6:23), emphasizing the relevance of thanksgiving in the conversion of scarcity into abundance.

This spiritual knowledge shows that the most sensible thing any of us can do is to constantly offer this sacrifice to God:

> "Therefore by [Christ] let us continually offer the sacrifice of praise to God, that is, the fruit of our lips, giving thanks to His name."
>
> —Heb 13:15

As Christians, we must emphasize joyful thanksgiving without making light of one another's difficulties:

> "Rejoice with those who rejoice, and weep with those who weep."
>
> —Rom. 12:15

As Paul also testified in 2 Corinthians:

> "Blessed be the ... Father of mercies and God of all comfort, who comforts us in all our tribulation, that we may be able to comfort those who are in any trouble."
>
> —1:3–4

To encourage a person in pain, we must enter spiritually into his or her hurt:

> "Bear one another's burdens, and so fulfill the law of Christ."
>
> —Gal. 6:2

But even in the roughest of times, we must exhort one another with sensitive encouragements to offer praise and thanksgiving, knowing that our Shepherd and King is deeply involved and has promised to act when we call:

> "Call upon Me in the day of trouble; I will deliver you, and you shall glorify Me."
>
> —Ps. 50:15

By calling on Him with the voice of thanksgiving, we number ourselves with the priests and the prophets and with all who "call upon Him in truth":

> "Oh, give thanks to the Lord! Call upon His name . . . Samuel was among those who called upon His name; They called upon the Lord, and He answered them."
>
> —Ps. 105:1; 99:6

We have repeatedly seen in scripture how praise and thanksgiving bind us to the Lord's name for the guarantee of His favor in our time of need. By the offering of thanks, we call on the Lord in truth, and we can confidently say with David:

> "The Lord will hear when I call to Him."
>
> —Ps. 4:3b

And:

> "In the day of my trouble I will call upon You, For You will answer me . . . For You, Lord, are good . . . And abundant in mercy to all those who call upon You."
>
> —Ps. 86:7, 5

We show the brokenness of absolute trust by offering thanks to the Father in times of pain and sorrow, knowing that He "is near to those who have a broken heart, And saves such as have a contrite spirit" (Ps. 34:18). By giving thanks to Him always, we show the humility of those whom He delights to deliver:

"I dwell in the high and holy place, With him who has a contrite and humble spirit, To revive the spirit of the humble, And to revive the heart of the contrite one."

—Isa. 57:15

The world of the unbelieving relies on its own wisdom and refuses the brokenness of grateful praise, but believers in Christ show the wisdom of salvation by falling before Him in joyful worship for the goodness of His word. As He says again in Isaiah:

"But on this one I will look, On him who is poor and of a contrite spirit, And who trembles at My word."

—66:2

In our seasons of pain we do not enjoy the hurt itself, but we rejoice in His assurance that "all things work together for the good of those who love God" (Rom. 8:28). The scripture tells us we should be "giving thanks always for all things," and "in everything give thanks" (Eph. 5:20). If we truly believe that "all things" work together for our good, we will gladly give thanks in "all things" (Rom. 8:28).

Under the old covenant law of sacrifice, the offerings brought to God had to be without blemish:

"And whoever offers a sacrifice . . . it must be perfect to be accepted; there shall be no defect in it."

—Lev. 22:21

"But if there is a defect in it, if it is lame or blind or has any serious defect, you shall not sacrifice it to the LORD your God."

—Deut. 15:21

A prayer offered without thanksgiving is defective. It is a sacrifice with blemish.

If your prayers have seemed dry and ineffectual, dash them with the salt of thanksgiving for a flavor well pleasing to God. By giving thanks to Him always, you will triumph in His praise, and like Daniel the prophet, you will walk among lions with no fear of harm.

# PART II

## A STORY FROM FRED MENDRIN'S LIFE

Fred Mendrin was born and raised in California's Central Valley, near Fresno. He attended Kerman High School, where he was active in three sports. In 1970, Fred was arrested for possession of half-an-ounce of marijuana with intent to sell, and he was sentenced to state prison with a term of six-months-to-ten-years. A year later, he joined a prison gang called the Aryan Brotherhood, and, in 1972, he committed a gang-related murder at a prison in Chino. For this crime, Fred received an additional sentence of seven-years-to-life. In 1978, he experienced a life-transforming faith in Jesus Christ as his Lord and Savior. He left the gang and the criminal lifestyle and committed his life to Christ.

Fred was paroled on September 1, 1985, and quickly became involved in jail and prison ministry. For many years he served as a volunteer for Prison Fellowship, which eventually hired him as a field director for the Central Valley. Fred currently holds the position of Prison Fellowship ambassador. He lives with his wife,

Liliya, and has three adult children, four grandchildren, and two great-grandchildren.

# CHAPTER 6

# DARE TO REJOICE

*"I smile at my enemies, Because I rejoice in Your salvation."*

—1 SAM. 2:1

## THE STORY

*In 2008, I suffered separation from Sue, my wife of more than twenty years. Nothing in my lifetime of ups and downs, of hard blows and disappointments, could have prepared me for separation from the woman my soul had been knit to and my dreams had been woven with. Sue had mothered my two beautiful daughters, who both had now grown and ventured out on their own. For so many years, after a day of work and ministry, I would come home to a house full of family, to the warm greetings, happy smiles, and tender hugs of the most special people. Suddenly, all of that was gone from my world.*

*During my years of marriage and raising children, I had not been physically abusive or unfaithful, and I had felt that I had done a good job of serving in ministry and providing for my* family. But now the reality was sinking in that I had forgotten how the beginning of a man's ministry is his own home. In the wisdom of God, "a man shall leave his father and mother and be joined to his wife," but I had left my father and mother to be joined to the church, with my wife and children in line after that. The marriage union is described in scripture as "a great mystery" designed by God to reflect the relationship of "Christ and the church" (Eph. 5:31–32), and by placing my out-of-home relationships in front of my wife and children, I had missed something fundamental in the glory of God's design.

For all of my focus on work and ministry, I had come up short with those whom Christ had made me the most responsible for. Now, each day at home, no one was there to greet me when I came in. No voices, no footsteps, no loving presence to welcome me. I would walk in through the front door and look around at the familiar furniture, like I was waiting for someone to come out of a room with a loving smile on a face that was glad to see me. But no one came out. I would walk into my bedroom and see that my wife's shoes were not on the floor and her clothes were not in the closet. I would look at the place on the bed where she slept, and the pillow where her head would rest next to mine at night, and I knew that I would sleep alone in that bed. When I would start to head out the front door, to leave for some place, no one was there to say, "Where are you going?" or "When will you be home?" For the first time since coming out of prison in 1985, I was alone.

Each morning, I left the house for my workday of washing windows at places of business, and all through the day I clung to Christ as my only refuge, my only hope. I felt like David when he had lost all, including his family, and even his own men "spoke of stoning him" (1 Sam. 30:1–6). I knew from scripture that David's history had been written "for our learning" (Rom. 15:4), and there was nothing left for me to do except, as David did, to "strengthen myself in the LORD my God."

Day after day, I went through my life under a mountain of agony, but clinging to God in prayer. At home, I began a habit of walking up behind a large reclining chair and falling to my knees. I would rest my forehead against the back of the chair and, there on my knees, with no other human to see or to hear, I poured out my soul to God and cried like a baby. That place behind the chair became my prayer closet.

One day, in confusion and agony, I said to the Lord, "Why are You allowing this to happen? I know You hate divorce!" In my mind I heard Him say, "I want all of you." I did not understand this. I knew that I was far from perfect in my walk with Christ, but since experiencing salvation by faith in a prison cell in 1978, the driving desire of my heart was to please and honor the Lord with my life. I said to Him again, with passion and agony in my voice, "I know that You hate divorce. Why are You letting this happen?" Again, I heard Him say in my mind, "I want all of you." After thinking about this for a minute, I expressed to the Lord, "Okay, Lord, I won't ask that again." Honestly, I did not know what this was going to mean, but I trusted my Lord to reveal all that I needed to know for Him to have everything He seeks in me.

My best friend and closest brother in Christ, Patrick Griffin, was in the state prison in Soledad. His phone calls and letters were always a comfort. He also had recently experienced a devastating experience of being denied release after an attorney assured him that he would be coming out. Patrick began sharing with me outlines that he had been developing on what the scriptures teach about praising God in all situations. One of the passages that he emphasized was from Second Chronicles, chapter twenty. Of course, I had read that chapter before, probably many times, but now the time had come for me to embrace why *the Holy Spirit had included that story in the Bible, and what it meant for me today.*

*The passage in Second Chronicles records a time when the king of Judah, named Jehoshaphat, was told that enemy armies were invading the land, and Jehoshaphat knew his small army stood no chance of turning back the large numbers that were coming to wipe out his nation. So, what did the king do in that situation? He confessed to the Lord that he had no strength of his own to fight against what was coming upon him, and that he did not know what to do. When I read this, I also confessed that I did not know what to do, and that my only wisdom was to call on the Lord for mercy and cling to Him as my hope and the meaning of my life.*

*In that history, recorded for my learning, the scripture describes how God instructed Jehoshaphat to place worshipers in front of his army as they went out to battle. He was also told that, although his army must go out to the battlefield, they would not need to fight, because the Lord would fight for them! Sure enough, when the army went out, as the singers lifted their voices in holy praise and thanksgiving to God, He turned the minds of the enemies against one another, and they wiped themselves out!*

*In my mind, I heard God speaking to me as I read what He said to Jehoshaphat: "Fred, you will not need to fight this battle. You have done all you could do, so just stand firm, hold your position, focus on joyfully praising and thanking Me, and see the salvation of the Lord on your behalf!" All through the day, I clung to that promise, believing that God had spoken it directly to me. While scrubbing windows, I focused on praising the Lord and thanking Him for His promise to take my battle into His own hand. I confessed my confidence that the outcome belonged to the Lord, and I reminded myself again and again to, "Stand firm, Fred. Stand firm!" The Lord kept me close to His breast, always encouraging me that this affliction is but for a moment. All through that day, and the next day, and the days and months that followed, my only wisdom was to cling to Christ. I had no other way to remain sane.*

*I knew that I needed to stay in fellowship with members of the Lord's body. I am an associate chaplain at the Fresno County Jail, and, at that time, I was leading a weekly Bible Study with about twenty inmates (whom we at Prison Fellowship refer to as "incarcerated citizens"). I shared openly with the men about the divorce process going on in my life, and the anguish I was suffering because of this. I had been asking for their support through prayer. One night, before a study, I poured out my soul to them like never before, and I asked if they would join me on their knees for prayer and worship. The men glorified God by kneeling and praying. I instructed them to praise God verbally, to raise their voices to the heavens! I was right there with them, singing and praising and thanking the Lord. From time to time, I paused to listen, feeling amazement as I heard these men in the jailhouse, down on their knees with their hands lifted high, shouting out to God, "I praise You, Lord God . . . I praise You, heavenly Father . . . I thank You and praise You, Lord Jesus!" What a joyous time we had, and I was mindful of the Psalm that says, "How good and pleasant it is For brothers to dwell together in unity! It is like the precious oil upon the head, Running down the beard, The beard of Aaron" (133:1–2). Yes, it was good for my soul to be in fellowship with the Body of Christ while offering up praises to my Lord, my Savior.*

*In a county jail, prisoners are still waiting for the outcome of their cases in court, living daily with the question of whether or not they will be sent to prison, or for how long. Naturally, this is a great mental challenge for county jail inmates, but after our time of worship on that night, I asked the brothers if their legal situations had been an issue in their minds while they offered praises to God? With warm and happy smiles they told me, one by one, that while they were joyfully praising and thanking the Lord, they were not worrying about their court cases. This illustrated what the Lord had been teaching me from His word and from experience, that fear and doubt cannot stand in the same room with praise. We were all learning that praise is an act of worship and a weapon of war.*

*For eight months, while the nightmare of the divorce process went forward, I dared to rejoice and put praise and thanksgiving in front of every care. Please do not think that I am claiming to have done this perfectly, but overall, by the grace of the Lord, I refused to stop praising Him, no matter how helpless I felt or how awful my situation looked.*

*Finally, the day came for Sue and I to meet at an attorney's office and sign the divorce papers. Like something out of a bad dream, I watched my hand signing the document that would legally end the marriage that I had once believed would last forever. After signing, I stood and said to her, "I'll see you." She nodded, and I turned and walked out the door. When I reached the parking lot, I felt the heaviness completely lifting, and I knew that I was going to be okay. The peace of Christ took hold of me in a more complete way than I had ever experienced. He had been with me and had brought me through those eight months of warfare, shepherding me through dark valleys when I felt overwhelmed and did not know what to do, showing that He takes seriously the beautiful truth that He, Jesus Christ the Son of God, is "the LORD my Shepherd" (Ps. 23:1).*

*After the divorce was finalized, I focused on my relationship with Christ and His will for me daily. I did not know if I would ever remarry, and it was not something I gave much thought to at all. But one day, in the summer of 2009, my sister Sandy told* me about a woman named Liliya who had moved to America from Ukraine and had worked for a short time as a caregiver for my parents. Sandy and Liliya had developed a good friendship, and the more my sister spoke about this lady, the more I became interested in meeting her.

One day, Sandy arranged for me to "just happen" to be in the area when she and Liliya got together for a girl-time at Starbucks in Clovis. When I "just happened" to be nearby, Sandy called and invited me to join them. I told her, "Sure, I'll be right over." After I arrived, the three of us talked for more than an hour, and I was amazed at how the beauty of the Lord emanated from Liliya. After our time together, as I pulled out of the parking lot, I looked through the passenger window at the table where they still sat, and Liliya was looking at me.

From that day, I knew deep in my heart that I wanted to get to know Liliya, and I prayed about this often, asking my heavenly Father to arrange another time for us to meet. This hope for a relationship with Liliya stirred my soul, and, four months later, the prayer was answered. It was a long four months, but the joy of the Lord was my strength all during that time. Praise to Him for His mercy that endures forever.

On New Year's Eve, going into the year 2010, I attended a gathering at a Russian Baptist Church where I knew that Liliya would be in attendance. We spoke only briefly, but after the service I went home and continued all night in prayer, pouring out my soul to my heavenly Father about Liliya, asking for wisdom, guidance, and assurance. At five in the morning, I sent her an email, sharing my desire to pursue a godly relationship. I do not remember her exact words, but I knew from her response that God had brought this delightful, godly, beautiful woman into my life to be my wife.

We began seeing each other regularly, and with Christ at the *center of our relationship, we grew together. One evening by a lakeside, with the moon reflecting off the still waters of Pine Flat Lake, I asked Liliya to marry me. She leaned into my arms without saying a word, and two days later, she told me, "Yes." On October 23, 2010, Liliya and I married.*

*Many years ago, when I was a young Christian in prison, we had a Bible Study about the ways in which God makes His love visible in our lives. Liliya is to me God's love made visible, His most visible daily evidence that the mercy of the Lord endures forever. I only need to look at her face to be reminded that no matter what is coming against me at any time, the greatest wisdom is to continue expressing my faith and hope in God by steadfast praise with joyful thanksgiving.*

*In summary, I want this part of my life story to illustrate that, in any situation, no matter how intimidating and drawn out it may seem, we are free to please God with the faith that moves mountains by daring to rejoice in Him.*

## BIBLE STUDY

Do you wonder how seriously the Father regards your prayers? Although you know that you are saved, does it seem that your voice is small in the kingdom of God? In this chapter, you will learn from the scriptures how the voice of rejoicing is delightful to the Lord, and you will learn how greatly you can honor Him at all times and in all situations. No matter how small or oppressed you have felt in the past, you can become an instant giant, walking in triumph, by the boldness of faith expressed in joyful praise.

\* \* \* \*

The reign of God is a rock of confidence for all who believe. The Bible records how Joseph's brothers had sold him into slavery:

> "Joseph—was sold as a slave. They hurt his feet with fetters, He was laid in irons. Until the time that his [God's] word came to pass, The word of the LORD tested him."
>
> —Ps. 105:17–19, brackets added

When Joseph gained the upper hand and his brothers approached him with trembling, he told them, "Do not be afraid . . . You meant evil against me; but God meant it for good" (Gen. 50:19–20). This example illustrates the bedrock of our confidence for rejoicing in even the worst of times: GOD OUR KING IS GOOD. Because He reigns, and because He is good, those who put their trust in Him will boldly rejoice in His name. As the scripture abundantly testifies:

> "The LORD reigns; Let the earth rejoice; Let the multitude of isles be glad!"
>
> —Ps. 97:1

> "Oh, clap your hands, all you peoples! Shout to God with the voice of triumph! For the LORD Most High is awesome; He is a great King over all the earth."
>
> —Ps. 47:1–2

Whoever approaches the Lord is expected to rejoice:

"Sing to God, sing praises to His name . . . And rejoice before Him."

—Ps. 68:4

In ancient kingdoms, a person risked execution for approaching the king with a sad expression, as this threatened the king's idea of himself as the provider of security, riches, and happiness for the subjects of his realm. The biblical writer Nehemiah recorded his fear after showing sadness at the table of King Artaxerxes (Nehemiah served as the king's cupbearer):

"Now I had never been sad in his presence before. Therefore the king said to me, 'Why is your face sad, since you are not sick? This is nothing but sorrow of heart.' So I became dreadfully afraid."

—Neh. 2:1b–2

His being "dreadfully afraid" shows the seriousness of his breach of culture, and although this custom in the presence of ancient kings was pretentious and vain, it helps to illustrate the proper way to approach the King of kings:

"Serve the LORD with gladness; Come before His presence with singing."

—Ps. 100:2

"Let us come before His presence with thanksgiving; Let us shout joyfully to Him with psalms."

—Ps. 95:2

Our joyful praise in the presence of God expresses delight in His goodness and confidence in His rule. But a failure to rejoice shows unbelief, and "without faith it is impossible to please Him" (Heb. 11:6).

The scripture tells us that, "Honor and majesty are before Him; Strength and gladness are in His place" (1 Chron. 16:27). If we truly aim to honor the Lord and to enjoy the fullness of His favor, we will rejoice before Him with passion and confidence in all situations.

The scripture in Romans tells us to "render therefore to all their due: taxes to whom taxes ... honor to whom honor" (13:7). Because God is the true and righteous King, all the earth is commanded to honor Him with joyful praises:

"Make a joyful shout to God, all the earth! Sing out the honor of His name; Make His praise glorious."
—Ps. 66:1–2

"Make a joyful shout to the LORD, all you lands!"
—Ps. 100:1

If you have felt small and irrelevant to the work of the kingdom, you can change this right now with the decision to "Break forth in song, rejoice, and ... Shout joyfully before the LORD, the King" (Ps. 98:4, 6).

The prophet Isaiah acknowledged to God that, "You meet him who rejoices and does righteousness" (Isa. 64:5). Do you want God's attention? You can have it immediately by lifting your voice and flooding his throne with "sacrifices of joy." This is how David brought his prayer to God's throne when "the wicked came against me to eat up my flesh" (Ps. 27:2):

"I will offer sacrifices of joy in His tabernacle; I will sing, yes, I will sing praises to the LORD. Hear, O LORD, when I cry with my voice!"

—Ps. 27:6–7a

David understood that the Lord "is a rewarder of those who diligently seek Him" (Heb. 11:6), and He delights to meet with those who seek Him joyfully.

If it seems your prayers have been met with silence, cry out to God with the voice of rejoicing and He will meet you with abundance.

Joyful praise is God's rightful due as the good Shepherd and the faithful King, and those who bring this delightful worship are the sons and daughters who live boldly by faith for the praise of His glory:

"This people I have formed for Myself; They shall declare My praise."

—Isa. 43:21

By joyfully praising God, we identify ourselves as the people who live in His presence, but a voice that refuses to rejoice in His name is not worthy of being heard at His throne.

David cried out in the wasteland of the wilderness, "My mouth shall praise You with joyful lips" (Ps. 63:5), and those who have faith will learn to live before God with joy at all times:

"In Your name they rejoice all day long."

—Ps. 89:16a

Not only in the day, but all through the night:

"Let the saints be joyful in glory; Let them sing aloud on
their beds."

—Ps. 149:5

Everything we say or do is to be offered to God through Christ
(Col. 3:17), but the offering must be accompanied with thanksgiving and joyful passion: "And whatever you do, do it heartily, as
to the Lord and not to men" (Col. 3:23).

This was the commandment given to Israel after the deliverance from Egypt:

"You shall rejoice before the LORD your God in all to which
you put your hands."

—Deut. 12:18

But Israel did not do this, and Moses prophetically warned:

"Because you did not serve the LORD your God with joy
and gladness of heart . . . therefore you shall serve
your enemies."

—Deut. 28:47–48a

By refusing to live with joy, we hand to our enemies a foothold,
but we can smile at adversity by rejoicing in the Lord. No matter
what the situation or how greatly the odds stack up against you,
the wisdom of scripture instructs you to "shout to God with the
voice of triumph!" (Ps. 47:1). Without leaving other things undone, step boldly into the day and believe the word that promises
we will "triumph in Your praise" (1 Chron. 16:35).

The enemy of faith is doubt, and it is doubt that hinders "the
power of God through faith" (1 Pet. 1:5) and keeps us away from
"the favor You have toward Your people" (Ps. 106:4). Are you

serving your enemies? If so, joyful praise is the way out. Whatever adversities and threats are coming against you, there is no opposition equal to God's power working through faith expressed in joyful praise.

The Lord "rules by His power forever" (Ps. 66:7a), and by rejoicing in Him we boldly express our delight in His goodness and our confidence in His power. There is no law to prevent you from rejoicing in Christ at all times "with joy inexpressible and full of glory" (1 Pet. 1:8).

When the shepherds of Bethlehem returned to their fields, they were "glorifying and praising God" after seeing the child whom the angel had announced with "good tidings of great joy" (Luke 2:20, 2:10). Have we allowed these tidings to grow stale in our hearts? Is there any legitimate reason for our joy in these tidings to diminish? If the birth of our Shepherd and King has become "old news" to us, we can experience the freshness of the tidings by rejoicing and giving thanks to the Father for the birth of the Son, singing songs of celebration to the glory of God from sunup till sundown and all through the night.

When the wise men came "from the East" to see Jesus soon after His birth, a miraculous star "came and stood over where the young Child was"; and when the wise men "saw the star, they rejoiced with exceedingly great joy" (Matt. 2:1, 2:9–10). If the wise men rejoiced with such joy after verifying the birth of the King, why should we not rejoice with even greater joy, since Christ is not only born but has also died for our sins and risen to reign forever?

Rejoicing is a weapon of warfare that strengthens our faith for pulling down strongholds, and our faith grows exceedingly bold as we offer the sacrifice of joy continuously. Regardless of our circumstances or the adversity in our lives, we should say with the prophet Habakkuk, "I will rejoice in the LORD, I will joy in the

God of my salvation." We should do this all day, any day, every day. We should do this because "the LORD Most High is awesome; He is a great King over all the earth" (Ps. 47:2).

But if we are not rejoicing in the word of the Lord, we show that we do not really believe it. A failure to rejoice is simply a failure of faith.

Joyful worship expresses our true identity in the righteousness of faith:

"The righteous shall be glad in the LORD, and trust in Him."
—Ps. 64:10

"Be glad in the LORD and rejoice, you righteous; And shout for joy, all you upright in heart."
—Ps. 32:11

We boldly show who we are by rejoicing aggressively in the name of Jesus, at all times and in all situations:

"Rejoice in the Lord always. Again I will say, Rejoice!"
—Phil. 4:4

"But let the righteous be glad; Let them rejoice before God; Yes, let them rejoice exceedingly."
—Ps. 68:3

By continual rejoicing, we embolden our faith for seizing the favor shown to the righteous, and as often as we remember His name, we should rejoice and give thanks:

"Rejoice in the LORD, you righteous, And give thanks at the remembrance of His holy name."

—Ps. 97:12

If your life is afflicted with adverse circumstances, you have all the more opportunity to glorify God with joyful praise, and to thank Him continuously as He takes control of your situation.

For a believer, circumstances do not determine the true quality of life on this passing earth. The world of the unbelieving will not agree because "the natural man does not receive the things of the Spirit of God, for they are foolishness to him" (1 Cor. 2:14). The apostle who wrote these words to the Corinthians also said in another letter:

"I have learned in whatever state I am, to be content. I know how to be abased, and I know how to abound. Everywhere and in all things I have learned both to be full and to be hungry, both to abound and to suffer need."

—Phil. 4:11–12

When Paul wrote this letter to the Philippian Christians, his body was burdened with chains and hemmed in by prison walls, and his problems were further compounded by allegations "supposing to add affliction to my chains" (1:16). In his lowly and painful circumstances, he beautified his life with joyful praise, showing by example how the truly good life is the one whose days are filled with rejoicing in Christ, no matter what the external conditions.

Paul exhorts us to not, under any circumstance, complain. Although no Christian can perfectly practice this, we are told in Philippians to "do all things without complaining and disputing, that you may become blameless and harmless, children of God without fault in the midst of a crooked and perverse generation, among whom you shine as lights in the world" (Phil. 2:14–15, emphasis added). By choosing to rejoice rather than complain, we mark ourselves as God's children who "shine as lights in the world." But when we complain, we are in defeat, giving ground to the enemy, failing as sons of the King.

A complaining person cannot say, "Through Your name we will trample those who rise up against us" (Ps. 44:5). A complaining person has forsaken the boldness of joy and is resisting "the power of God through faith" (1 Pet. 1:5). Complaining is a show of unhealthy faith, or of no faith at all, since a person cannot complain and walk in faith at the same time.

The voice of complaining belongs to the world of unbelief, but the power of God works through a voice that thunders with faith.

The scripture exhorts us to "take up the whole armor of God. . . and having done all, to stand" (Eph. 6:13). We do not stand by complaining. We stand by joyful faith that exalts the word of God.

If your life is assaulted by problems beyond your strength and understanding, dare to put the praise of rejoicing ahead of everything. No matter how absurd your joyful faith might appear to the world around you, sing to God with steadfast rejoicing, and He will vindicate your confession.

By endurance in rejoicing we run strong to the finish:

"But none of these [tribulations] move me; nor do I count my life dear to myself, so that I may finish my race with joy."
—Acts 20:24, brackets added

By racing with joy, we make our whole life a sprint to the crown of glory that waits at the finish.

The scripture in Romans describes the kingdom of God as a

realm of "joy in the Holy Spirit" (Rom. 14:17), teaching us that rejoicing in Christ is the culture of the kingdom and that faith without joy gives only a partial experience of the fullness of life in Christ.

For those who have biblical faith, the true value of life is centered in praise and not in external conditions. By a lifestyle of joyful praise, our conditions become our servant as the power of God works through faith to bring abundance from scarcity, never doubting that the desert will blossom as we fill our days with rejoicing from beginning to end. Although we are thankful for pleasant circumstances and we should aggressively pursue opportunities to enrich the lives of others in the name of Jesus, the true source of our joy is not in passing pleasures but in "the word of our God" which "abides forever" (1 Pet. 1:23).

"[H]e who is of a merry heart has a continual feast" (Prov. 15:15), and there is no circumstance that can threaten the feast of those who rejoice in the Lord "as one who finds great treasure" (Ps. 119:162). As Paul also instructed by example: "Everywhere and in all things . . . rejoice in the Lord" (Phil. 4:12; 3:1). When we live without joy, we will struggle with unhealthy faith, but by filling our hearts with joyful faith, we have an endless feast.

The scripture tells us in Proverbs:

> "Anxiety in the heart of man causes depression, But a good
> word makes it glad."
>
> —12:25

The good word is Jesus Christ, from Genesis through Revelation. And for those who believe in Him, there is no excuse for defeat, because the Almighty God our Father has authorized us to rejoice.

If your life is dry, intimidating, or painful, there is no law to prevent you from leaping for joy at God's treasure in Christ (Gal. 5:22–23). There is no law to prevent you from joyfully celebrating "as men rejoice when they divide the spoils or as those who rejoice "according to the joy of harvest" (Isa. 9:3). There is nothing at all to prevent you from launching immediately into a life of joyful triumph through constant praise in the name of Christ. By continually offering songs of joy, your life will become a sustained celebration of the Father's glory in the Son.

In the world, you will have adversity, but in a stressful situation there is no better policy than to joyfully sing to God.

If your spirit is dull and your life is oppressed, you will experience a dramatic change on every front by filling your days with the sacrifice of joyful praise. Regardless of how small and painful your life has felt, exalt the Lord with joyful song, and the Father of mercies will meet you richly with the favor that He shows to the righteous.

Twenty centuries ago, a virgin gave birth to the Son of God, and, several decades later, He died for our sins and rose to the Father's right hand, where He leads as our Shepherd and reigns as our King. Through the boldness of faith, you can joyfully celebrate the day of His birth, and you can rejoice exceedingly in the day that He was seen alive from the dead. You can rejoice with those whom He healed and be glad with those whom He raised, and you can joyfully walk with Him in the wind and the rain on the waves of the sea.

# PART III

## A STORY FROM DONNALEE'S LIFE

# CHAPTER 7

# REJOICING THROUGH SORROW

*"The sacrifices of God are a broken spirit,*
*A broken and a contrite heart—*
*These, O God, You will not despise."*

—Ps. 51:17

## THE STORY

*On October 16, 2016, my husband, Patrick, sat in front of a committee that would decide if he should be paroled. I remember waking up in the morning with happiness that this day had finally come. It was a Friday, and I knew that I would see him the next day in the visiting room, where we hoped to rejoice together in the wonderful news that he would soon be coming home to me. Patrick's sister, Pam, had driven up to Soledad from Orange County the night before, so that we could spend the day together in front of the prison in prayer and worship. It was a day of great expectation for all of us.*

*The hearing was scheduled for 8:00 in the morning, so we drove to the prison early and parked near the railroad tracks across the street from the entrance gate. We could not go onto the prison grounds, so we made that little area by the tracks our worship center. We got out of the car and immediately lifted our hands in joyful praise. For the next four hours, we worshiped non-stop, thanking and praising God in the name of Jesus Christ, waiting for Patrick to call from the prison yard and let us know the decision. Of course, we joyously hoped for news that he was coming home, but we wanted to do all we could to express to God our commitment to worship Him no matter what the outcome of the hearing.*

*As the hours passed, we felt the heat of the day and the draining of energy in our bodies, but we kept on praising God, walking around the car with our hands lifted and our voices offering songs and other expressions of joyful thanksgiving. I was fifty-four years old at the time, and Pam is three years older, but the Lord gave us energy to continue the offering. Finally, at noon, we sat down to rest our bodies and wait for the call. Less than a half hour passed, and my phone sounded. I answered on the first ring and turned on the speaker so Pam could share in the moment. My breathing was strong with excitement as I leaned forward in my seat to hear Patrick's voice coming on, and then I heard him say that he had been **denied** parole.*

*I do not remember exactly what Patrick said. I only remember how his words tumbled into my soul like heavy stones, pounding me down and down and down. Although I had tried so hard to prepare for any kind of news, in my deepest soul, I had expected to hear my beloved tell me he was coming home. When he told me the opposite, I felt shock and disbelief. A denial meant that we would need to wait at least three more years before he would have another hearing, and after all that I had already been through, the pain of the disappointment seemed like more than I could really handle. But, in that same moment, I heard in my spirit the word of the Lord, assuring me that He has plans to prosper me and not to harm me. After the initial moments of feeling traumatized, I fled back to worship. I confessed to my heavenly Father that I was not going to let anything keep me from lovingly praising Him. The Lord had prepared both Pam and I for this, to be ready to praise God with all our hearts, no matter what news Patrick brought us. So, I did that, focusing my mind on worship, but after a few minutes, the power of the hurt began pulling me back the other way. For the rest of the day, I experienced that back and forth, using the weapon of praise to fight the enemy of doubt. I wish that I could say that I flawlessly triumphed all the way through. I really wish that I could say that, but the truth is that my triumph was a forward stumble rather than a steady march of victory.*

*Shortly after receiving the news, Pam left for her five-hour drive home. I spent the next few hours alone in my studio apartment, fighting with all my heart to stay true to my promise to God that I would keep worshiping Him no matter what. I also knew that I would have company that night. What happened is that, once or twice a month, I would open my apartment to women who had driven a long distance to visit their men in the prison, to save them the high cost of renting a motel in a prison town. Since my apartment was so tiny, I rarely allowed more than one guest, but on that night, there would be two. I would have preferred to be alone, but I saw it as an opportunity to show them how life in Christ goes on, even when carrying a mountain of pain.*

*My guests arrived a little after sundown, and I welcomed them graciously. I told them they could sleep in the bed, and I would use a mattress on the floor in the kitchen. After we had talked a while, I went alone into the kitchen to begin preparing sandwiches for ministry to the homeless in the Chinatown section of Salinas (about thirty miles away). This is a ministry that the Lord had enabled me to begin soon after moving to Soledad in 2014, and I became well known to the people in Chinatown. They called me "The Church Lady"; and as soon as they saw my car, they would gather around it as I got out and opened my trunk for them to select from the clothes, shoes, and other items that had been donated in the surrounding towns. Then, I would distribute the little sack lunches with sandwiches, cookies, and one or two other food items. This ministry gave me an awesome opportunity to speak to the people about Christ Jesus, and I have many special memories of my times there. So, on that night in my apartment, while my guests talked with each other a few feet away, I focused on worship as I made the sandwiches.*

*Whenever I stopped worshiping, the arrows of doubt and fear came flying at my mind. Sometimes I would even start mentally accusing my husband, thinking he had done something at the hearing to deliberately make them decide to not let him out. I had met Patrick in 2013, and a year later I moved from Salt Lake City to Soledad, to marry him and to support him in every way that I possibly could. He had been in prison since 1979 and had been walking with the Lord since 1981. I believed in the sincerity of his faith and love for Christ, but as I stood in the kitchen making sandwiches, I seriously wondered if he had been in prison so long that he really did not want to come out. I started thinking that because I am so good to him, visiting him every weekend, paying for phone calls and always being there for him, maybe I am helping him feel so comfortable that he would rather stay where he is than come out and deal with life on the outside.*

*While standing there in the kitchen, I was thinking things like*

*that. Then, after a few minutes, I would feel conviction and re-*
*pent from the doubt, fear, and anger, and I would return to wor-*
*ship. Back and forth it went, and later that night, as I struggled*
*to fall asleep on my floor-mattress, I clung to Christ in adoring,*
*trusting praise. For all my ups and downs since getting that call*
*from the prison, I had kept stumbling forward, and I closed out*
*the night in the triumph of praise.*

*In the next chapter, I will share the outcome, not just on the*
*following day when I saw my husband in the visiting room, but*
*years later, when the Lord favored us with an amazing deliver-*
*ance. I want to close this part of my story by acknowledging that*
*sometimes our grief can be so severe that we simply do not feel*
*like praising God, and even the thought of joy can seem unrealis-*
*tic and almost insulting. In times like these, it is so important to*
*remind ourselves that God is stronger than our pain, and, as the*
*scripture says, "when I am weak, then I am strong" (2 Cor. 12:10).*

## BIBLE STUDY

Is your grief so severe that you can no longer relate to the experience of joy? Have the blows of loss and failure left you unsure
that a better life is even possible? In this chapter, you will learn
from biblical examples how your suffering can become an offering to God, who is deeply involved for your good. We will look
at scriptures that assure us the Lord "is near to those who have
a broken heart" (Ps. 34:18), and how the sacrifice of a broken
spirit will never be turned away at the throne of Almighty God.

\* \* \* \*

Jesus, "who for the joy that was set before Him endured the

cross" (Heb. 12:2), demonstrated the power of joy that comes through faith no matter how dark the hour. The prophet Isaiah described Him as "a Man of sorrows and acquainted with grief" (Isa. 53:3), but Jesus spoke also of a joy that the world cannot experience, a joy found only in Him by those who abide in His word:

> "These things I have spoken to you, that My joy may remain in you, and that your joy may be full."
> —John 15:11

Jesus described this fullness of joy as something the world cannot take away, saying to the disciples on the night of His betrayal:

> "Therefore you now have sorrow; but I will see you again [after three days in the grave] and your heart will rejoice, and your joy no one will take from you."
> —John 16:22, brackets added

When Jesus spoke this way about the joy experienced by those who believe, the Lord Himself was "sorrowful and deeply distressed," saying to the disciples in the garden of Gethsemane:

> "My soul is exceedingly sorrowful, even to death."
> —Matt. 26:38

But He had just finished a prayer in which He said:

> "I come to You, and these things I speak in the world, that they may have My joy fulfilled in themselves."
> —John 17:13

While "exceedingly sorrowful," Jesus prayed that all who

believe would experience the fullness of joy that filled His own heart. This is "the joy of the Lord" that comes only through faith in the assurance that "all things work together for good to those who love God" (Rom. 8:28). Because Jesus perfected obedience, He rejoiced with perfect assurance that His suffering was an instrument through which enormous good would be accomplished, and we who believe also have access to this wellspring of joy through faith in His righteous name.

In the exhortation to worship with joyful praise at all times, we do not make light of sorrow. "Jesus wept" (John 11:35), and in this world of pain we, too, will weep. But we do not sorrow with "the sorrow of the world" (2 Cor. 7:10); instead, we offer our tears with joyful cries of gratitude for God's promise of good through all that we suffer. A Christian trained in the scriptures will show tender respect for pain and sorrow while encouraging the sufferer to cast his burden on the Lord by joyfully giving thanks. As James tells us:

"My brethren, count it all joy when you fall into various trials."
—James 1:2

But sometimes the trials are "beyond measure," and in times such as these we face the question of: How far can we live by faith? Is there a limit? Do you feel that your pain and loss are just too much? Does it seem unreasonable to even think of rejoicing? In your great trial of pain, you will need to decide whether the word of God is always true, or only sometimes true.

When Job was hit with the pain of enormous loss, he "fell to the ground and worshiped. And he said: '. . . The LORD gave, and the LORD has taken away; blessed be the name of the LORD'" (Job 1:20–21). Controversy has sometimes swirled around this passage in Job, but we know with biblical certainty that when Job made this statement, he "did not sin nor charge God with wrong" (1:22). Although we cannot explain the full mystery, we know that our God is somehow involved for our good in the tragedies we suffer.

In a season of great sorrow (his children were killed), Job did not give pleasure to Satan by doubting the goodness of God. He did not "charge God with wrong," but acknowledged that the goodness of God was stronger than his pain and would somehow prevail to the praise of His glory if Job would stay faithful. Job, the suffering saint, declared his righteousness by offering praise in a time of tragic distress, and the scripture later testifies how "the LORD blessed the latter days of Job more than his beginning" (Job 42:12).

However great your pain, and however deep your loss, you can reach out to God with tears on your fingers and rejoice with confidence that His word of promise is stronger than your grief.

Praising God in a time of sorrow is not a "positive mental affirmation." It is a bold confession of faith in the goodness of God and in His faithfulness to shepherd our lives through the hardest of times. The great lesson of Job's experience is summarized in the Book of James, showing us once again that, in times of trial, we can reach with our pain for the word of assurance that God is involved for our good:

> "Indeed, we count them blessed who endure. You have heard of the perseverance of Job and seen the end intended by the Lord—that the Lord is very compassionate and merciful."
>
> —5:11

As Christians, we do not endure adversity with "gritted teeth." Rather, in times of sorrow, we worship through tears and "give thanks to Your holy name, to triumph in Your praise" (1 Chron. 16:35). But only the mind of faith can reason with the logic of joy in a time of great affliction.

Peter also wrote to Christians under trial, saying in his first epistle:

> "In this [salvation] you greatly rejoice, though now for a little while, if need be, you have been grieved by various trials."
>
> —1:6, brackets added

Although these Christians were "grieved by trials," they continued to "greatly rejoice," and Peter applauds their faith when he writes in the same passage:

> "Jesus Christ, whom having not seen you love. Though now you do not see Him, yet believing, you rejoice with joy inexpressible and full of glory."
>
> —1:7b–8

In the grief of trial, they rejoiced exceedingly in the Lord's promise to accomplish good through all that they suffered. While showing full respect for the pain of affliction, they encouraged one another with assurances of faith in the goodness and power of God.

Sorrow is legitimate for Christians in a passing world, but as we develop our spiritual understanding, we learn to walk on stormy water with our eyes fixed on Jesus. The heart of a growing believer is a sponge, absorbing the joyful presence of Christ and praising Him with confidence for the favor He shows to those who come boldly. We do not rejoice in the suffering itself. We rejoice in our Lord's assurance that every tear is in His book, and no adversity can separate us from His loving promise to order all things for our good. By having the boldness to rejoice while in the greatest pain, we march through our days in the power of triumph as "more than conquerors through Him who loved us" (Rom. 8:37).

The scripture guarantees triumph through a lifestyle of praise, which leads also to good works in greater abundance. A life of fruitfulness is not what saves us; rather, this is the purpose for which we are saved (Titus 2:14; Eph. 2:10; John 15:8). Whatever comes against you, no matter how hurt or how hopeless you feel, cling to God in praise and live with confidence in all He has promised through Jesus our Lord.

The apostle Paul repeatedly demonstrated this strength of joy in difficult times, saying in Colossians: "I now rejoice in my sufferings for you" (1:24). And in Second Corinthians: "I am exceedingly joyful in all our tribulation" (7:4b). As he said also to the Christians in Thessalonica:

"And you became followers of us and of the Lord, having received the word in much affliction, with joy of the Holy Spirit."
—1 Thess. 1:6

The Book of Hebrews was written to Christians who "endured a great struggle with sufferings . . . and joyfully accepted the plundering of your goods" (10:32, 10:34). Their unpleasant experience of being plundered provided opportunity for glorifying God by rejoicing in a time of distress. These Christians would not have enjoyed the suffering itself, but, with boldness of faith, they rejoiced with confidence that "the LORD is my Shepherd" and "I shall not want" (Ps. 23). These afflicted believers were exhorted to "hold fast the confidence and the rejoicing of the hope firm to the end" (Heb. 3:6), being assured that God "is a rewarder of those who diligently seek Him" (Heb. 11:6).

Sorrow and affliction are no threat to the joyful faith of those who live boldly for Christ, as Paul testified yet again when he spoke of being "sorrowful, yet always rejoicing" (2 Cor. 6:10). When the Lord said to Paul in a time of infirmity, "My strength is made perfect in weakness" (2 Cor. 12:9), Paul rejoiced in this word so boldly that even his weakness became an avenue for the power of Christ:

> "Therefore most gladly I will rather boast in my infirmities, that the power of Christ may rest upon me. Therefore I take pleasure in infirmities, in reproaches, in needs, in persecutions, in distresses, for Christ's sake. For when I am weak, then I am strong."
>
> —2 Cor. 12:9–10

Paul had previously viewed his infirmity as an obstacle to the fullness of life, telling us how he had "pleaded with the Lord three times that it might depart" (2 Cor. 12:8). By learning to "take pleasure" in his infirmity, the power of Christ multiplied in Paul's life and ministry, not because he enjoyed the distress of the infirmity, but rather because he rejoiced in the assurance that "all things work together for good to those who love God" (Rom. 8:28). By rejoicing through times of great affliction, he brought to maturity the faith by which all things are possible, and even his afflictions became an instrument of power for the edification of many to the glory of God.

If you are spiritually discouraged because of infirmity, or adversity, or failure in your life, be encouraged to know the one-step remedy for chronic spiritual weakness is the leap into a lifestyle of praising God. Fear and depression, discouragement and sorrow, cannot stand in the presence of praise. As the psalmist says again:

> "Why are you cast down, O my soul? And why are you disquieted within me? [He has slipped into worry and depression, but he knows the remedy] Hope in God; For I shall yet praise Him, The help of my countenance and my God."
>
> —Ps. 42:11, brackets added

The power of God works through faith, and the walk of faith is purified by continual rejoicing. By feeding the heart with joy, our faith takes wings to say with the persecuted psalmist: "By my God I can leap over a wall" (Ps. 18:29). And with the imprisoned apostle: "I can do all things through Christ who strengthens me" (Phil. 4:13). And with Mary, before the physical evidence of the promise: "He who is mighty has done great things for me" (Luke 1:49).

All of these believers rejoiced in God's word "as one who finds great treasure" (Ps. 119:162), and none of these accepted the idea that adverse circumstances can threaten the Lord's ability to perform what He has promised. In the face of doubt, they joyfully shouted, "Let God be true, but every man a liar" (Rom. 3:4). This is the faith that moves mountains and causes human feet to walk on water.

Our Lord assured us that "in the world you will have tribulation" (John 16:33a). The triumphant life of exceeding joy is no cakewalk for the flesh, as Paul affirmed in describing the pilgrimage of those who learned through scripture and through experience to "rejoice in the Lord always" (Phil. 4:4):

"For we do not want you to be ignorant, brethren, of our trouble which came to us in Asia: that we were burdened beyond measure, above strength, so that we despaired even of life. Yes, we had the sentence of death in ourselves, that we should not trust in ourselves but in God who raises the dead."

—2 Cor. 1:8–9

And:

"We are hard-pressed on every side, yet not crushed; we are perplexed, but not in despair; persecuted, but not forsaken; struck down, but not destroyed."

—2 Cor. 4:8–9

Are you hard pressed and baffled? Do you feel struck down and torn on the inside? You can make your pain an offering to God by sacrifices of praise for His promise of good through all that you suffer. Even in the hardest of times, you can worship through tears and overcome the world by joyful shouts of confidence in the name of Jesus.

When the power of grief has crushed your vision of what could still be possible, and when pain and helplessness leave you small and with no sense of adequacy for the demands of life, you can lift up your soul to kiss the words of Him who spoke of joy while He was "exceedingly sorrowful, even to death" (Matt. 26:38). You can do this because the Lord is your Shepherd and He is with you. You can do this in the darkest hour of the coldest night. You can do this right now.

# CHAPTER 8
# REJOICING WITH SONG

*"Therefore, I will play music before the LORD!"*

— 2 Sam. 6:21

## BIBLE STUDY

Are you struggling with spiritual motivation? Do you have addictions that cripple your spiritual life? Or do you simply feel inadequate for the work of ministry among the needy people of your community? In this chapter, you will learn how the offering of song results in spiritual growth and mighty outpourings of "the power of God through faith" (1 Pet. 1:5). No matter where you are or what your situation, the Holy Spirit will take control of your life as you offer "psalms and hymns and spiritual songs, singing with grace in your hearts to the Lord" (Col. 3:16).

\* \* \* \*

When Paul and Silas had received "many stripes" and been thrown "into the inner prison" with "their feet in the stocks," they sang to God "with the voice of triumph" that shook the earth and shattered the chains (cf. Acts 16:22–26; 2 Cor. 2:14; Ps. 47:1). All of this was "written for our learning" (Rom. 15:4) to show us how all things are possible for those who live by "the power of God through faith" expressed in songs of praise.

To make a noise to God in the name of Christ is an aggressive show of confidence and affection, and believers are often urged in scripture to "make a joyful shout to God" (Ps. 66:1). The following verses bring emphasis to the boldness of faith expressed in making a joyful noise to celebrate the Father's glory in the Son:

"Shout joyfully to the LORD, all the earth; Break forth in song, rejoice, and sing praises."

—Ps. 98:4

"Sing to God, sing praises to His name."

—Ps. 68:4

"Make a joyful shout to the LORD, all you lands!"

—Ps. 100:1

"Oh, let the nations be glad and sing for joy!"

—Ps. 67:4.

"[L]et Your saints shout for joy."

—Ps. 132:9b

"Blessed are the people who know the joyful sound!"

—Ps. 89:15a

"Praise Him with loud cymbals; Praise Him with clashing
cymbals! Let everything that has breath praise the LORD."
—Ps. 150:5–6

By songs of praise we offer to God the fullness of worship,
as when the priests under the old covenant were appointed "to
offer the burnt offerings of the LORD . . . with rejoicing and with
singing" (2 Chron. 23:18). With shouts and songs, as well as by
quiet melody in the heart, you will perfect your offering to the
Father through Jesus, and the song within you should be for Him
and Him alone. As the psalmist confessed:

"Therefore my heart greatly rejoices, And with my song I
will praise Him."
—Ps. 28:7

God has ordained music as a powerful expression of faith and
love, and if you seriously desire to "grow in the grace and knowledge" of Christ (2 Pet. 3:18), you will fill your heart continually
with "psalms and hymns and spiritual songs" (Eph. 5:19).

Believers should be cautious about music that does not aim
to celebrate the goodness of God and "His wonderful works to
the children of men" (Ps. 107:21). It is the nature of the case
that worldly music identifies with the god of this world, and a
Christian places his or herself at enormous spiritual risk by receiving into the mind what is knowingly "not of the Father but is
of the world" (cf. 1 Jn 2:15–17). Each of us must decide what we
will do, but there is no godly wisdom in throwing open the doors
of the mind to the seductive influence of music that does not aim
to celebrate our Savior and King. Jesus said, "He who has an ear,
let him hear what the Spirit says to the churches" (Rev. 3:6). But

can we hear the Spirit of God while our hearts are filled with the music of the world?

We, as the Lord's people called to a lifestyle of praise and thanksgiving, should not be naïve to the spiritual danger of yielding our minds to a sound that exhibits enmity toward God by its friendship with the world (cf. James 4:4).

The prophet Isaiah spoke of how cultural harlotry is promoted through music:

> "Take a harp, go about the city, You forgotten harlot; Make sweet melody, sing many songs, That you may be remembered."
>
> —Isa. 23:16

The songs of the harlot called to remembrance the pleasures of sin, and to receive her music is to be stirred by her spirit. Each of us can choose to listen or not to listen, but none of us can choose to escape the consequences of willfully absorbing the spirit of an unbelieving world.

A Christian who feels a need to enjoy the world's music does not have a developed understanding of the joy of making music to the Father through Jesus. Wherever you are, on a hiking trail or a hospital bed, a lakeside park or a prison cell, you can be "filled with the Spirit" by rejoicing with "psalms and hymns and spiritual songs, singing and making melody in your heart to the Lord" (Eph. 5:18–19).

But can any of us truly glorify the Lord while our hearts are filled with the songs of this age?

Isaiah warns us through the Spirit against music that stimulates ungodly thinking and conduct:

"The harp and the strings, The tambourine and the flute, And wine are in their feasts; But they do not regard the work of the LORD, Nor consider the operation of His hands."

—Isa. 5:12

A musical experience that does not exalt "the work of the LORD" has no legitimate place in the creation of God. The scripture commands "all the earth" to "break forth in song, rejoice, and sing praises" (Ps. 98:4), but the voice of the world refuses to praise, and it darkens the mind through music that suppresses the knowledge of God.

If your life has been dry and unfruitful, you may need to assess your level of involvement with the world. Are you where you want to be spiritually? None of us are, but one thing we can do is put away the things that compromise us. The power of God works through faith, and "all things are possible" (Mark 9:23) to those who believe without doubting. If you are eager for the power of God to move mountains in your life, you will need to embrace the scriptures that instruct us to drive away doubt and worldliness by filling our hearts with continuous songs of praise.

The scripture exhorts us to associate the meaning of life with praise, and to invest every moment with eternal value and with resurrection power by joyfully singing to God. As David vowed:

"I will sing to the LORD as long as I live; I will sing praise to my God while I have my being."

—Ps. 104:33

For David, the value of each moment was its opportunity for bringing glory to God with songs of praise. And if we expect to triumph through God as David did, we will sing as David sang.

Not because singing itself has magical value, but simply because God has ordained song as a primary expression of the worship through which union with the Creator is experienced.

Because song is so fundamental to the spiritual act of worship for the glory of God and the good of man, the god of this world exploits the mental impulse of song to celebrate rebellion, unbelief, and death. If the allurement of worldly music has been a snare for you, you can deaden its influence by aggressively filling your heart with songs of joyful praise. "Whoever offers praise glorifies Me" (Ps. 50:23), and as you cultivate in your mind a habitual pattern of spontaneous song, you will experience the power of the Spirit in ways that you had not imagined.

Songs of joy express the faith by which all things are possible, as David wrote in a psalm for "the chief musician" when "the LORD delivered him from the hand of all his enemies" (18:1):

> "For by You I can run against a troop, By my God I can leap over a wall."
>
> —18:29

When walls of opposition surround you, leap into your day with songs of praise and sing with passion in the night:

> "[I]n the night His song shall be with me— A prayer to the God of my life."
>
> —Ps. 42:8

By songs of praise, we lay hold on His strength and confess our confidence in His mercy:

"I will sing of Your power; Yes, I will sing aloud of Your mercy in the morning . . . To You, O my strength, I will sing praises; For God is my defense, My God of mercy."
—Ps. 59:16–17

The Bible shows how the people of God recorded His exploits in songs to be learned and handed down, as when the Lord provided Israel with water at a place they called *Be-er* ("Well"):

"Then Israel sang this song: 'Spring up, O well! All of you sing to it— The well the leaders sank, Dug by the nations of nobles, By the lawgiver, with their slaves.'"
—Num. 21:17–18

There are many examples of this in the biblical history, but each of us can devise our own songs to celebrate the beauty and the exploits of the Lord that we ourselves have witnessed:

"Come and hear, all you who fear God, And I will declare what He has done for my soul. I cried to Him with my mouth, And He was extolled with my tongue."
—Ps. 66:16–17

"Sing to Him a new song; Play skillfully with a shout of joy."
—Ps. 33:3

"I will sing to the LORD, Because He has dealt bountifully with me."
—Ps. 13:6

Each one of us is authorized to offer songs that commemorate how the Lord "has dealt bountifully with me," and by filling our hearts with creative songs, we "worship God in the Spirit" (Phil. 3:3) with sacrifices of delightful fragrance:

> "May my meditation be sweet to Him; I will be glad in the LORD."
>
> —Ps. 104:34

> "I will praise the name of God with a song, And will magnify Him with thanksgiving. This also shall please the LORD."
>
> —Ps. 69:30–31

When you feel the urge to do something good and pleasant, you can break out in song to God:

> "For it is good to sing praises to our God."
>
> —Ps. 147:1

> "Sing praises to His name, for it is pleasant."
>
> —Ps. 135:3

Does your life seem dull? Are you trapped in an ugly circumstance, surrounded by boredom with no end in sight? You can beautify every moment and make it last forever by investing the moment with praise.

The scripture tells us that "the eyes of the LORD run to and fro throughout the whole earth, to show Himself strong on behalf of those whose heart is loyal to Him" (2 Chron. 16:9). Do you have cares that you are helpless to do anything about? A son or a daughter in the military? A runaway child whose whereabouts you do not know? The scripture guarantees the Lord's involvement as you keep your heart loyal to Him, and there is no better way to fix your heart on God than to joyfully sing His praise. By worshiping Him with song and thanksgiving, you can know with joyful certainty that, wherever on earth you have a care, the eye of the Lord is there to show Himself strong on your behalf.

Do not underestimate the reach of His power or the beauty of His mercy. Without leaving other things undone, cast all your cares on Him by "singing and making melody in your heart to the Lord." By offering songs of joyful worship, you have put your cares into the hand of the living God, and what better place could you possibly put them?

The scriptures so abundantly emphasize the beauty of song in the worship of God and the quality of life:

"Sing to Him, sing psalms to Him; Talk of all His wondrous works!"

—1 Chron. 16:9

"Sing out the honor of His name."

—Ps. 66:2a

"Shout joyfully before the LORD, the King."

—Ps. 98:6b

"Sing to the LORD a new song, And His praise from the ends of the earth."

—Isa. 42:10

"We will sing and praise Your power."

—Ps. 21:13

By rejoicing in His power, we experience His power. As David sang "when he fled from Saul into the cave":

"I will cry out to the LORD Most High, To God who performs all things for me . . . I will sing and give praise."

—Ps. 57:2, 7

In a time of absolute helplessness, you can boldly say, "The LORD will perform all things for me while I sing and give praise." We should never forget the example of Jehoshaphat when the kingdom of Judah faced impossible odds. The scripture records how the king "appointed those who should sing to the LORD . . . as they went out before the army" (2 Chron. 20:21). Having done all that he could [he sent out the fighters], Jehoshaphat put the singers ahead of it all, and "when they began to sing and to praise, the LORD set ambushes against [the opposition]; and they were defeated" (20:22, brackets added).

Are you facing great opposition? Are you chained to addictions or restricted by a difficult circumstance? Do you feel dry in your spirit and insufficient for the work of ministry? The remedy for you is to sing to the Lord day and night. You do not need a long course on spiritual recovery. You do not need to climb a tall staircase of spiritual steps. You need to praise God.

The scripture assures us:

"God has gone up with a shout, The LORD with the sound of a trumpet. Sing praises to God, sing praises! Sing praises to our King, sing praises! For God is the King of all the earth."

—Ps. 47:5–7a

If we truly believe that God is the King, we will understand the value of praise, and the scripture exhorts us to "sing praises with understanding" (Ps. 47:7b). By faith, we understand through the scriptures that God has ordained praise "to silence the foe," and by constantly praising God, you will turn the tables on every adversity in your life.

Do not let the stones take your blessing. Sing to the Lord with joyful songs, and refuse to stop, knowing from the scripture of truth and from historical example that the Lord will take control of your life if you come to Him boldly with songs of thanksgiving. By shouts and songs and "melody in your heart to the Lord" (Eph. 5:19), you will glorify Him with joyful faith as you march through your days in the triumph of praise.

## THE STORY

*As I struggled to fall asleep on the kitchen floor, I focused on worship through music. Over and over I mentally sang two of my favorite songs. One is by Kari Jobe and is titled "I Am Not Alone." In that song of adoring faith in Christ are the words, "I am not alone, I am not alone, You will go before me, You will never leave me." The other song is "Trust in You," by Lauren Daigle, with lyrics that go something like this:*

> *When You don't move the mountains*
> *I'm needing You to move*
> *when You don't part the waters*
> *I wish I could walk through*
> *when You don't give the answers*
> *As I cry out to you*
> *I will trust, I will trust,*
> *I will trust in You!*

*Over and over and over I focused my spirit in worship with the words and the melody of those powerful songs. Each time I woke up during the night, even when it was just for a minute to turn from one side to the other, those songs played in my mind. In the morning, the moment I opened my eyes, the songs were still there, fresh and alive. Even when I was not consciously trying to sing, the lyrics played inside of me, and I stepped forward into my day with music as my offering of praise and my weapon of war.*

*My guests left for the prison an hour before me, and as I pre-pared for the visit with my husband, again and again my situation pressed so heavy on me that I broke down in tears. Alone in my apartment, I could let it all out in the presence of the Lord, cling-ing to Him in worship with songs in my heart and on my lips. I have read in scripture of how God works through spiritual mu-sic, like when the prophet Elisha received no vision until he in-structed his servant to offer a song (2 Kings 3:15), or when God worked through David's music to drive an evil spirit away from King Saul (1 Sam. 16:23). In my fight against doubt and fear, un-certainty and loneliness, sadness and confusion, I can honestly say the Holy Spirit used those spiritual songs to pull me through.*

*At about nine o'clock, I opened my door and paused to turn and look back at the small room. This is something I did almost every day during my years in that apartment. I gave thanks to God for my pillow and my bed, and for everything I could see in the room, including my grandbabies whose pictures lined the walls. Then I asked the Lord for protection over my dwelling while I was gone, and I stepped out and closed the door. As I walked on the sidewalk in the narrow space between the apartment build-ings, I looked up at the sky and thought of my husband and what he must be going through in that very moment. Each time I felt I was about to cry, I just focused on worshiping with song. I reached my car and got inside, feeling the heat of the day already rising, and I started my drive to the prison about two miles away,* to the same noisy little visiting room which was the only place on earth where I had ever seen the face of my husband.

At the prison, after the long process of finally getting into the visiting room, I went to the podium to find out which table my husband and I would be assigned for the day. For the next few minutes, as I purchased items from the vending machines for us to enjoy when he arrived, others in the room were approaching me and telling me how sorry they were to hear that Patrick had been denied parole. Each time that someone approached me with this, I would nod and say something like, "Thank you for caring and showing your kindness, but I can assure you that God has a reason for this, and that He is going to bring something awesome out of it." Whenever I said this to someone, I truly meant it, and I knew this painful experience was all part of His plan to bring good to my house.

After I had set up our table with drinks and snacks and the *Study Bible* which the inmate workers in the visiting room always kept to the side for us (because we had used that same Bible every weekend for years, and it was filled with our handwritten notes on so many of the pages), I looked up and saw my beloved walking toward me. As soon as I saw him, I wanted to cry, and it would have been okay if I had, but instead I wanted to show him the strength the Lord was showing me. We threw our arms around each other and hugged and kissed, then sat down and went into prayer. After that, we shared our deep emotional experience, and then we took everything to the word of God. We ate and drank from the living scriptures where the voice of Christ reminded us, again and again and again, that He is the one who opens what no one shuts, and shuts what no one opens, and that the meaning of our lives is to be pleasing to Him, no matter what is coming upon us. Then, we sang together. Not just one song, and not just two. Patrick is not known for his singing skills, but *his voice sounded so beautiful to me, and I knew that our voices were beautiful to God.*

*As we concentrated on worship instead of on what was hurting us, our spirits rose and rose. When the visiting hours ended, after I kissed my husband and we clung to each other for as long as the rules allowed, I walked out into the parking lot with my husband still in the prison, and I knew that our God was going to use this experience to prepare us all the more for our life of ministry together when He does bring Patrick out of the prison.*

*That afternoon I took my guests with me to Chinatown, where they helped me distribute the lunches and where I joyfully shared the Gospel with the needy who have no homes. I told them about homes that can never be destroyed, and where thieves cannot break in and steal, and how they can have such a possession by repenting from the hopelessness of life without Christ, and fleeing to Him as their Savior and Lord. The next day, I had another wonderful time with my husband, with the Spirit ministering to us so powerfully through one another. Then the weekend was over, and our eyes were fixed on Christ whom we trusted to shepherd us through the years until Patrick's next parole hearing. We had walked together through a devastating experience, answering every stab of pain with a song of praise. We did not know that only seventeen months later, Patrick would be called back early for another hearing, and, on August 24, 2018, he would walk out through the gates to put his loving arms around me in the prison parking lot, with Fred and Liliya Mendrin and my sister-in-law, Pam, standing joyfully with us.*

*As Patrick and I type these words of true history onto the page, I am sitting next to my beloved in our home on the top of a hill, worshiping God together in the triumph of praise.*

*Patrick and I now have our own version of the song by sister Lauren Daigle, with the additional words:*

*Lord, You have moved the mountains*
*That we asked You to move*
*And You have parted waters*
*For us to walk through*
*And You have truly answered*
*When we cried out to You,*
*And we thank, and we thank,*
*and we thank You, Lord!*

*Truly, the Lord has done this for us, but when it seemed He was **not** moving the mountains or parting the waters, He gave us the grace to praise Him still.*

# REVIEW INQUIRY

Hi, this is Patrick and Donnalee!

We hope you have enjoyed the book, finding it both useful and encouraging. We have a favor to ask.

Would you consider giving Stories of Praise a rating wherever you bought it? Online book stores are more likely to promote a work when they feel good about its content, and reader reviews are a great barometer for a book's quality.

So, please go to the website of wherever you bought this, search for our name and the book title, and leave a review. If you are able, perhaps consider adding a picture of you holding the book. That increases the likelihood your review will be accepted!

Many thanks in advance,

Patrick & Donnalee Griffin

Special bulk discounts are available. If you would like your whole team or organization to benefit from reading *Stories of Praise,* contact FredSMendrin@gmail.com or visit Acts29Ministry.org.

# WOULD YOU LIKE PATRICK GRIFFIN TO SPEAK TO YOUR ORGANIZATION?

## BOOK PATRICK NOW!

Patrick accepts a limited number of speaking engagements each year. To learn how you can bring the Acts29 message to your organization, email FredSMendrin@gmail.com or visit Acts29Ministry.org.

# ABOUT THE AUTHORS

**Patrick Griffin** is the lead writer of autobiographies for two successful Fresno businessmen as well as for a motivational speaker on the John Maxwell Leadership Team. At age twenty-three, Patrick experienced a life-transforming faith in Jesus Christ while preparing to commit suicide in his cell in a California state prison. Although he did not parole until age sixty-one, he used those years to develop his skills for research and writing, along with personal growth and deep involvement in prison ministry. At age fifty-five, he received from God the miracle gift of his wife, Donnalee, who works as his assistant in research and writing projects. He and his wife are members of non-denominational Inner City Christian Fellowship in San Diego, where he serves as a teacher and mentor under Pastor Mark Seramur. Patrick and Donnalee live with their two beautiful cats in a family-owned house in Southern California.

**Donnalee Griffin** has co-written three published books with her husband, and also works part time as a professional caregiver for the elderly. She is the author of *How God Remembers Me.* Donnalee is the youngest of thirteen children and was raised in Bayshore, Long Island, New York. Her childhood experience of scarcity helped to later develop in her a deep passion for individuals who are challenged with basic survival needs, such as those without homes. From 2014 to 2018, while waiting for her husband's release from prison, she started and maintained a food and basic-care ministry to provide help to the homeless in the Chinatown section of Salinas, California. She loves sharing the testimony of Christ Jesus and doing Bible Studies with her husband and other family and church members. Also, one of her greatest joys is FaceTiming with her grandchildren in Florida.

Patrick and Donnalee can be reached at: Acts29Ministry.org.

Made in the USA
Las Vegas, NV
12 August 2021